독립獨立 없는 해방解放은
시리도록 아프다

고산지의 장편 서사시

Liberation without Independence Left Painful Sores

고 산 지 지음
이 기 태 영역

독립 없는 해방은 시리도록 아프다

배문사

추천서문

고산지 시인의 장편 서사시집《독립없는 해방은 시리도록 아프다》의 추천사를 부탁받고 거절하기 어려웠다. 고산지 시인은 현재 본인이 이사장으로 있는 '국제 PEN 한국본부'의 이사로서, 본인과 함께 활동하고 있다.

고산지 시인의 말에 의하면 1970년대 후반 (주)경방에 재직 중이면서 '시인의 집'에서 시작詩作 활동을 시작했으며, 한국청년학교(대림재건학교)에서 불우 청소년을 가르쳤다고 한다. 당시 그는 긴급조치 9호 위반으로 두 번에 걸친 가택 수색 등 안기부와 보안사의 내사를 받았다고 한다. 격동의 1980년대 광주에 내려가 기업가企業家로 변신한 그는 1990년대 회사가 도산倒産하자 일본으로 건너가서 50개월 동안 불법 체류하면서 잡역부(노가다) 생활을 했던 의지적 인물이다. 그의 일본에서의 불법체류 삶은《차명借名의 세월》이라는 간증 일기로 출간되었다.

IMF가 나던 해 일본에서 귀국한 고산지 시인은 망우동에서 의정부로 이사하였다. 2000년대 전세유민傳貰流民으로 의정부에 정착한 그는 의정부영락교회에 적籍을 두고 믿음 생활을 계속하였다. 2010년 부도난 지 20여 년만에 신용불량자에서 복권復權된 그는, 마침내

의정부 영락교회의 시무장로로 피택되었다. 이런 그의 삶 때문이어선지 고산지 시인은 자신의 삶이 하나님의 은혜였음을 친구들에게 즐겨 고백하였다. 그리고 나에게 "대한민국의 건국建國은 하나님의 역사였다."고 말하곤 하였다.

1882년 9월, 임오군란 당시 명성 황후의 목숨을 지킨 공으로 수신사 박영효의 비공식 수행원이 되어 일본에 간 이수정은 "Boys be Ambitious for Christ"로 유명한 클라크 박사의 제자인 농학자農學者 쓰다 센(津田仙)을 만났다. 거실의 벽에 걸린 족자에 쓰인 "虛心者福矣 以天國乃其國也(마음을 비운 자는 복이 있도다. 천국이 그의 나라가 될 것이니 - 마태복음)"라는 글은 그를 그리스도 앞으로 인도하였고, 일본에서 세례받은 첫 한국인 개신교 신자가 되었다.

이수정은 일본 유학 중 마가복음을 한글로 번역하였다. 언더우드 선교사와 아펜젤러 선교사는 이수정이 번역한 마가복음을 들고 조선에 입국하였다. 이 후 발간된 한글 성경은 교회뿐만 아니라 일제하에서 문맹퇴치 및 여성의 지위 향상과 민족의 자존심을 일깨우는데 큰 공헌을 하게 되었다. 1919년 3 · 1운동당시 기독교인은 전체 인구비율중 1.3%인 20만 명에 불과했지만 독립선언 33인의 서명인중 15명이 기독교인이였다. 또한 3.1운동에 참여하고 투옥된 9,458명중 2,087명이 기독교인이였다.

하지(John Reed Hodge) 장군의 통역관인 윌리엄스(George Zur williams) 중령(한국명: 우광복禹光復)의 등장은 우연이 아닌 '여호와 이레' 의 필연이라고 주장하는 고 시인의 주장에 나는 반론을 제기할 수가 없다. 제2차 세계 대전 이후 해방된 대부분의 신생국은 소련의 영향을 받아 공산화 되었지만, 아시아에서 유일하게 자유 민주주의 체제를 지키고 있는 국가가 바로 대한민국이기 때문이다. 한국 현대사의 뜨거운 감자인 1945년 8월 15일부터 1948년 5월 31일까지의 정치적 상황을 사실에 입각해서 서사시로 노래하고 있는 시집 《독립 없는 해방은 시리도록 아프다》의 마지막 장 이윤영 의원의 기도문은 제헌국회의 속기록에 그대로 남아 있다.

이 시집이 큰 울림이 되어 수많은 사람을 깨우치는 사명使命을 감당하는 귀한 시집으로 사랑받기를 기도하면서 고산지 시인의 건강, 건필을 기원한다.

2018년 10월 22일

국제PEN한국본부 이사장 손 해 일

Contents

차 례

Liberation without Independence Left Painful Sores

Prologue

We couldn't claim our country as a homeland while even robbed our language and our own names.

God saw and heard our circumstances in which we had to suffer to live as citizens of the Japanese Imperialists for 36 years.

God did a great thing by protecting our nation until that day when the East Sea's waters run dry and Mt. Baekdu is worn away.

The blessed news of liberation came like dreams, mountains and rivers were dancing and the rocks were singing.

As our tongues were set free and our mouth could call our names

독립獨立 없는 해방解放은 시리도록 아프다

프롤로그

조국祖國을 조국이라 주장하지 못하고
우리 말과 우리 이름을 빼앗긴 채

황국신민皇國臣民으로 살아온 36년 간의 고통을
그분이 보셨네, 그분이 들으셨네

동해물과 백두산이 마르고 닳도록
보우하신 하나님이 큰 일을 행하셨네

꿈결같이 찾아온 해방의 복된 소식
산천이 춤을 추고 돌들이 노래했네

우리 혀가 풀리고
우리 입이 우리 이름 부르니

We thought it was merely a dream.
It seemed like we were dreaming.

Our stolen language was restored and we could call our names at high voice.

It seemed like we were dreaming.
We thought it was a dream.

Although the freedom of liberation was not a real independence

Lots of people indulged in freedom talked as they thought, behaved as they thought.

Those who forgot that it was done by God's great grace
Thought it was by their own power and acted at their will.

We had to plough and sow with sweat,
They slandered one another divided into left and right wing.

We had to be united under one holy light,
Light up lamp in the East.

꿈결인 줄 알았네
꿈꾸는 것 같았네

빼앗긴 언어 회복되고
빼앗긴 이름 목청껏 부르니

꿈꾸는 것 같았네
꿈결인 줄 알았네

해방解放의 자유自由가
독립獨立이 아닌데도

자유에 도취된 수많은 사람들
소견대로 말하고 소견대로 행동했네

하나님의 크신 은혜 망각한 사람들
제 힘으로 된 줄 알고 마음대로 행동했네

땀 흘려 씨 뿌리며 기경起耕해야 했는데
좌, 우로 갈라져 서로를 비방했네

We could not get over the high wall of ideology,
Our nation was divided into North and South.

연합하여 하나 된 거룩한 빛으로
동방의 등불을 밝혀야 했는데

이념理念의 벽 넘지 못해
남북南北으로 갈라졌네

Eve of Liberation of the Nation

We had no power to spin ourselves
In the swirl of upheaval,
We sacrificed our whole body and soul
And borrowed the whip of the great powers
To turn the wheels of history
Many of us disappeared into the mists of time.
We had no power, no power at all
Even though we tried our best day and night
At the very place where we fell down
In order to save the country overcoming the shame
We had no power
No power of our own.

Though we fought against Japanese army
By crossing the Yalu River and the Tumen River
For the independence of our fatherland
Even wandering here and there in despair
In the foreign land China.
However, we couldn't recover our land even an inch by our own power.

Nazism, fascism and Japanese militarism
Oppressed the freedom of individual

해방전야解放前夜

격변의 소용돌이 속에서
스스로는 회전할 힘이 없어
열강의 채찍을 빌려서
역사의 수레바퀴를 돌리고자
온 몸을 바친 사람들
세월의 뒤안길로 사라지고
그들이 넘어진 자리에서
수치羞恥를 딛고 나라를 찾기 위해
불철주야不撤晝夜 혼신의 노력을 다 했으나
우리에겐 힘이, 힘이 없었네

압록강을 건너 두만강을 넘어
중국 대륙을 떠돌며
조국의 독립을 위해
일본군과 싸웠으나
우리의 힘으로는 나라 땅을
한 뼘도, 한 뼘도 수복할 수 없었네

민족과 국가의 존립, 발전을 위해 인간이 존재한다는

Under the totalitarian ideology.
Under the theory that individuals exist for the existence of nation and its development,
And the Allied countries that fought for democratic values,
Their post war processing for the defeated countries
Lead to a system of confrontation between capitalism and socialism.

The standards of negotiation between the nations were not based on justice.
Their own domestic profit was the basis for negotiations.

The Soviet Union was the largest beneficiary country in Europe before and after the war.

In all over the region of Eastern Europe, a totalitarian system so-called peoples' democracy was introduced under the guidance of the Soviet Union.

Many senior Korean communists disappeared by purge
In the process of the Stalin's Great Purge went on.

Soon after the disappearance of the senior Korean communists
Stalin prepared the war against Japanese imperialism. He developed partisans struggle.

전체주의 이념 아래 개인의 자유를 억압하는
나치즘과 파시즘, 일본의 군국주의와
민주주의 가치를 내세우며 싸웠던 연합국의
패전국敗戰國에 대한 전후戰後 처리 문제는
자본주의資本主義와 사회주의社會主義의
체제 대립으로 이어졌네

국가 간의 협상 기준은 정의正義가 아니었네
자국自國 이익이 협상의 기준이었네

전후戰後 유럽의 최대 수혜국受惠國은 소련이었네

동유럽의 모든 지역에는 소련의 지도하에
인민 민주주의로 불리는 전체주의 체제가 들어섰네

수많은 원로 한인 공산주의자들은
스탈린의 대숙청 과정에서 사라졌네 **「註釋*1」**

원로 한인 공산주의자들이 사라지자
스탈린은 일본 제국주의와의 전쟁에 대비하여
빨치산 투쟁을 전개하면서
동유럽과 같은 소련의 위성 국가를 세우기 위한
군사, 정치 지도자의 양성을 목적으로

He founded the 88th Reconnaissance Brigade in June 1942.
To train military and political leaders
With aim of building the Soviet satellite countries like Eastern Europe.

In June 1945, the 88th Reconnaissance Brigade,
They declared the completion of the task of training course.

U.S president Franklin D. Roosevelt believed that
The imperialist nations took only honey from the colonies
And they did not contribute to the people,
Devised a new method of trusteeship instead of dissolving the overseas colonies after the war.

His aim was to make the colonies to be independent when they have an ability of self-independence by investing in the areas of education, welfare and social indirect capital.

Roosevelt thought Korea would take 20～30 years
Until the days of taking autonomous ability
Considering the Philippines case which took 50 years
After taking control over it in the wake of the US-Spanish War.

About the report of 〈Chicago Sun〉 that US president Franklin Delano Roosevelt adopted trusteeship as US policy on the issue of post war matters, Rhee Syng-man sent a violent tone of protesting letter to the US government on March 15, 1942.

88정찰여단을 창설했네(1942. 06.)「註釋*2」

1945년 6월, 88정찰여단은
지도자 훈련 과정의 과업 완성을 선언했네

제국주의 국가들이 식민지의 단물만 빼먹고
주민들에게는 기여한 바가 없다고 생각한
루즈벨트(Franklin Delano Roosevelt) 대통령은
전후 해외 식민지를 해체하는 대신
새로운 신탁 통치 방법을 구상했네

식민지에 교육, 복지, 사회 간접 자본 투자를 하여
자치 능력이 생기면 독립시키는 방법이었네

루즈벨트는 미·스페인 전쟁을 통해 지배권을 넘겨받은
필리핀의 자치 독립이 50여 년 걸렸듯이
한국도 자치 능력을 갖기까지는
2~30년의 신탁 통치가 필요하다고 판단했네

전후 처리 문제에 대해 루즈벨트 대통령이
신탁 통치안信託統治案을 미국의 정책으로 채택했다는
〈시카고 썬(Chicago Sun)〉지의 보도에 대해
이승만李承晩은 격렬한 어조의 항의문을

The first document that referred to the post-war Korean independence was Roosevelt's letter to Jiang Jie-shi via Jiang Jie-shi's political advisor, Owen Lattimore on December 24, 1942.

"The new trusteeship plan can be applied to the colony
In addition to the returning the autonomic power to the colony after the war."

"It is not desirable to resolve the independence issue of Korea without involvement of the Soviet Union. Should the Soviet Union be isolated, it promotes tension rather than alleviating tension."

President Roosevelt told British Foreign Minister Anthony Eden
Upon his visit to Washington on March 27, 1943 offered his opinion:

"With reference to the post-war disposition of Japan's colonial and occupied territory?
He referred again to the independence policy of Korea, upon defeat of Japan, The trusteeship will be assumed to 3-4 countries including the United States and China."

In the Cairo declaration, three persons Roosevelt, Winston Leonard Spencer Churchill and Jiang Jie-shi agreed upon on November 27, 1943:

미국 정부에 보냈네(1942. 03. 15.) 「註釋*3」

전후 한국 독립을 언급한 첫 번째 문서는(1942. 12. 24.)
장제스蔣介石의 정치 고문 오원 래티모어(Owen Lattimore)를
통해 장제스에게 보낸 루즈벨트의 서신이었네

"전쟁이 끝나면 식민지를 종전의 식민지 국가에 되돌려
주는 것 외에 새로운 신탁 통치 방안을 적용할 수 있다."

"조선의 독립 문제를 소련의 관여 없이 해결하는 것은 바람직
하지 않고, 소련을 고립시키는 것은 긴장을 완화하기보다는
긴장을 조장하게 된다."

1943년 3월 27일, 워싱톤을 방문한
영국의 이든(Anthony Eden) 외상에게 루즈벨트 대통령은

"일본의 식민지와 점유지에 대한 전후 처분과 관련하여
한국의 독립 방침을 재차 언급하면서, 일본 패망시 한국의
신탁 통치를 미국과 중국을 포함한 3~4개 국에 위임한다."
는 의견을 제시했네

카이로 선언에서 루즈벨트와 처칠(Winston Leonard Spencer
Churchill) 장제스蔣介石 등 3인은(1943. 11. 27.)

"We need to bear it in mind that Koreans are now under slavery status,
In accordance with the proper procedure in the future, we agreed to give the freedom and independence to the Korean people."

Rhee Syng-man and Korean Provisional Government requested
To the US government to clarify what does it mean by 'proper procedure'
But there was no answer.

When Roosevelt attended at the Teheran talks on November 28, 1943 announced;

"Korean people need about 40 years of probation period before they gain complete Independence."

When Italy surrendered on September 8, 1943, the Allied Powers got meetings in Cairo, Yalta and Potsdam.

They discussed on the issue of post-war in Europe and Asia.
The United States insisted to have forty years of trusteeship,
But the British and the Soviet Union were against it
And no agreement was made.

In Yalta talks on February 11, 1945,
Roosevelt told to Losif Vissarionovich Stalin
That Korea would need 20 to 30 years of trusteeship
If considering the past experience of governing the Philippines.

"현재 조선인이 노예 상태 아래 놓여 있음을 유의해
앞으로 적절한 절차에 따라
조선인에게 자유와 독립을 줄 것"에 합의했네

이승만과 임시 정부는 선언문 중
'적절한 절차에 따라'가 무엇을 의미하는지
미정부에 해명을 요구하였으나 응답이 없었네
「註釋*4」, 「註釋*5」

테헤란 회담(Teheran Conference)에 참석한
루즈벨트는(1943. 11. 28.)

"조선인은 완전한 독립을 얻기 전에 약 40년 간의 수습 기간
이 필요하다."
고 발표했네

이탈리아가 항복하자(1943. 09. 08.)
연합국은 카이로와 얄타, 포츠담 회담에서
유럽과 아시아에 대한 전후 처리 문제에 대해 협의했으나
40년 간의 신탁 통치를 주장하는 미국의 주장에
영국과 소련이 반대하여 합의할 수 없었네

Roosevelt officially asked Stalin to participate in the Pacific War
Under the condition that South Sakhalin and Kuril Islands that Japan occupy
To be transferred to the Soviet Union
Within three months of German surrender.

After President Roosevelt who led the trusteeship plan
Suddenly died on April 12, 1945.
Vice president Harry S. Truman took over the presidency.

When Germany surrendered on May 7, 1945, the four nations which won the war, they established the Allied Management Committee on June 5, 1945 in Berlin.
They issued a joint declaration on the divided governing of Germany,
And joint management by the four countries based on the agreement of the Yalta Talks.

At the Potsdam talks on July 26, 1945,
The three leaders of the US, British and Soviet Union
Agreed on four principles;
Germany's disarmament, demilitarization, getting out of Nazis and democratization.
Upon writing the Potsdam Declaration on Japan,
Jiang Jie-shi of China also joined.

They demanded Japan to surrender under the same conditions.

얄타 회담(Yalta Conference)에서(1945. 02. 11.) 「註釋*6」
루즈벨트는 스탈린(Iosif Vissarionovich Stalin)에게
필리핀을 지배한 경험에 의하면
조선은 20~30년 동안은 신탁 통치를
실시해야 할 것이라고 설명했네

루즈벨트는 일본이 점령하고 있는
사할린 남쪽과 쿠릴 열도를 소련에 양도한다는 조건으로
독일 항복 후 3개월 이내에 태평양 전쟁에 참전해 줄 것을
스탈린에게 공식적으로 요구했네

신탁 통치안信託統治案을 주도했던
루스벨트 대통령이 갑자기 서거(1945. 04. 12.)한 후
부통령 트루먼(Harry S. Truman)이 대통령직을 승계했네

독일이 항복하자(1945. 05. 07.) 전승戰勝 4개 국은
베를린에 연합국관리위원회(1945. 06. 05.)를 설치하고
얄타 회담 합의에 근거하여 독일의 분할 통치와
4개 국 베를린 공동 관리에 관한 공동 선언문을 발표했네

포츠담 회담에서(1945. 07. 26.) 「註釋*7」
미국, 영국, 소련 3국의 정상들은
독일의 무장 해제와 비무장화, 탈 나치 및 민주화라는

However, the Japanese army insisted on keeping their National Seal,
And they emphasized to preserve their national status.
Japan finally held two hands on the dropping two times of atomic bombs
In Hiroshima on August 6, 1945 and Nagasaki August 9, 1945.

Stalin delayed to participate in the war
On account of the mutual non-invasion treaty with Japan, he declared the war on August 9, 1945, after the atomic bomb fell on Nagasaki.
He ordered his soldiers to advance to Manchuria and North Korea.

On August 15, 1945, Japanese king Hirohito
Accepted the Potsdam declaration and declared the unconditional surrender.

When Germany was divided into East and West Germany
Japan wanted to prevent the division of the Japanese archipelago
Japan proposed to the US Forces Command that
Manchuria to be occupied by China and Japan to be occupied by the United States.
And suggested the Korean peninsula to be divided into two parts
North and South of the 38th parallel

And the Japanese forces in the Northern part to be surrendered to Soviet Union.
And the Japanese forces in the Southern part to be surrendered to the United States.

네 가지 원칙에 합의했네
일본에 대한 포츠담 선언문 작성시에는
중화민국의 장제스도 합류하였네

동일한 조건으로 일본에게 항복을 요구한
포츠담 선언문에 대해
국체 수호國體守護를 강조하며
옥쇄玉碎를 주장했던 일본 군부軍部도
히로시마(廣島, 1945. 08. 06.)와 나가사키(長崎, 1945. 08. 09.)에
투하된 두 발의 원자 폭탄에 손을 들고 말았네

일본과 맺은 상호 불가침 조약을 이유로
참전參戰을 미루던 스탈린은
나가사키에 원폭이 투하되자
선전 포고와 함께(1945. 08. 09.) 소련군에게
만주와 북한으로 진격을 명령했네

1945년 8월 15일, 일왕 히로히토裕仁는
포츠담 선언을 수락하고 무조건 항복을 선언했네

패전 독일이 동, 서독으로 분할되자
일본은 일본 열도의 분할을 막고자
만주는 중국, 일본은 미국이 점령하고

The United States accepted this Japanese proposal,
And they decided the 38th parallel line of the Korean peninsula
As a military demarcation line between US and Soviet Union Army
To make the Japanese Army surrender and demilitarize.
Thus the south of the 38th parallel line was occupied by the US and the north by the Soviet Union Army.

The surrender of Japan was signed on board the aircraft carrier Missouri anchored in Tokyo Bay on September 2, 1945.
It was surrender to the members of the Allies; The United States, the Soviet Union and China.

It was not Japan's surrender to Korea.

Jiang Jie-shi who was defeated by the Communist Party of Mao Zedong fled to Taiwan.

A surrender document of Japan was delivered to him on September 3, 1945.

The People's Republic of China commemorates the day when the Japanese surrender document
was delivered to Jiang Jie-shi of the Republic of China as the Anniversary of a Victory.
However, we, Koreans had even no piece of Japanese surrender papers.

한반도는 북위 38선을 경계로
북한 주둔 일본군은 소련에게 항복하며
남한 주둔 일본군은 미국에 항복할 것을
미군 사령부에 건의했네

이를 수락한 미국은 일본군의 항복과 무장 해제를 위하여
한반도의 38도선을 미, 소 양군의 군사 분계선으로 확정하고
38선의 이남은 미군이, 이북은 소련이 점령했네

1945년 9월 2일, 도쿄만東京灣에 정박한 항공모함
미주리 호(Missouri 號) 선상에서 조인된 일본의 항복은
연합군의 일원인 미국과 소련, 중국에 대한 항복이었네

한국에 대한 일본의 항복이 아니었네

마오쩌둥毛澤東의 공산당에 패해
타이완臺灣으로 밀려난 장제스에게
1945년 9월 3일, 일본의 항복 문서가 도착했네

중화민국 장제스에 일본의 항복 문서가 도착한 이 날을
중화인민공화국은 전승절戰勝節로 기념하고 있지만
우리는 왜곡할 만한 항복 문서조차 갖지 못했네

When the military administration was executed by the US Army that occupied South Korea,

There was a subtle movement between the US Army that is willing to maintain split occupation policy and the US State Department that is pursuing international trusteeship policies.

한국을 분할 점령한 미군美軍의 군정軍政이 실시되자
분할 점령 정책을 유지하려는 미 육군성과
국제 신탁 통치 정책을 추진하고 있는 미 국무성 사이에
미묘한 움직임이 감지되었네

Preparatory Committee for Founding of A Nation

Liberation was not achieved
By my hands, by our hands!
Freedom in painful sores!
Oh, the rivers and mountains of our fatherland!

Freedom came to us but in the political circumstance of liberation,
We couldn't decide our destiny by ourselves in the ideological turmoil.
The liberation allowed no order.

As Japan's defeat became clearer
Abe Nobuyuki, governor of the Choseon Dynasty
Proposed to Song Jin-woo to transfer the sovereign power.

Song Jin-woo simply rejected Japan's proposal
Stating that the transfer of sovereignty is meaningless
Should the winning country, US does not approve it.

The second negotiator, Yeo Wun-hyung accepted the proposal of

The governor and as soon as Japan surrendered on August 15
He launched the 'Preparatory Committee for the Founding of Choseon'

건국준비위원회

내 손으로, 우리 손으로
이루지 못한 해방解放이여
시리도록 아픈 자유自由여
조국祖國의 산하山河여

질서의 자유가 아닌 이념의 혼돈으로
이 땅을 찾아온 해방 정국解放政局에서
우리는 우리의 운명을
스스로 결정할 수 없었네

일본의 패배가 확실해지자
아베 노부유키阿部信行 조선 총독은
송진우宋鎭禹에게 통치권 이양을 제안했네

승전국인 미국이 허락하지 않는
통치권 이양은 의미가 없다면서
일본의 제의를 일언지하一言之下 거절한 송진우

When serious cracks occurred between a part of nationalists and communists
Who participated in the Preparatory Committee for the Founding of Choseon,
Yeo Wun-hyung offered bargaining to Ahn Jae-hong
To cooperate with the nationalist line.

On that night when Yeo Wun-hyung offered bargaining,
He got terror in the alley in front of his house on August 17.
It was for the first time after liberation.

The meeting of the National People's Representatives was opened by the Preparatory Committee for the Founding of Choseon on the 6th of September.

They elected 55 members of the National People's Representatives
Who hold concurrent position of the Committee Member of Draft Law Maker and elected 12 advisors.
They enacted the Provisional Organization Law of the People's Republic of Korea, and established 'The People's Republic of Korea (PRK)

Those who set up the People's Republic of Korea on September 7 appointed Rhee Syng-man as head, Yeo Wun-hyung as deputy head and Hu Hun as prime minister.

두 번째 협상 대상자 여운형呂運亨은
총독부의 제안을 받아들이고
8월 15일 일본이 항복하자
'조선건국준비위원회朝鮮建國準備委員會' 를 발족시켰네「註釋*8」

조선건국준비위원회〔建準〕에 참여한
민족주의 계열 일부와 공산주의 계열 내부에서
심각한 균열龜裂이 발생하자
여운형은 민족주의 계열과의 합작을 위해
안재홍安在鴻에게 담판을 제안했네
그날 밤 여운형은 자택 앞 골목길에서(1945. 08. 17.)
해방 후 최초로 정치를 테러당했네 「註釋*9」

전국인민대표자회의를 소집한 건준建準은(1945. 09. 06.)
헌법 기초 위원을 겸직하는
55명의 전국인민대표위원과 12명의 고문을 선출하여
「조선인민공화국임시조직법」을 제정하고
'조선인민공화국朝鮮人民共和國' 을 수립했네 「註釋*10」

건준을 해체 조선인민공화국을 수립한 이들은
주석에 이승만李承晩, 부주석에 여운형
총리에 허헌許憲을 추대하여 임명했네(1945. 09. 11.)

Song Jin-woo, Kim Sung-soo and Jang Duck-soo, who belong to nationalist group insisting the respect of the Provisional Government, waited for the returning home of Shanghai Provisional Government, didn't recognize the organizing of the People's Republic of Korea.

The US Military Government announced a statement denying the reality of the People's Republic of Korea on October 10.

Rhee Syng-man who returned to Korea also refused to take the position as head on the 16th of October.

임정 봉대론臨政奉戴論을 주장하며
상하이 임시 정부의 환국을 기다리던
민족주의 계열의 송진우, 김성수金性洙, 장덕수張德秀 등은
조선인민공화국의 조각組閣을 인정하지 않았네

미 군정이 조선인민공화국의 실체를 부인하는
성명을 발표했네(1945. 10. 10.)

환국한 이승만도 주석 취임을 거절했네(1945. 10. 16.)

The Beginning of Military Government 1

Thick darkness covered the Korean peninsula.

The seed of the gospel that conceived the light even in the thick darkness
Was germinated by the churches owing to the campaign to abolish illiteracy
And the enlighten movement.

Missionary William B. McGill was
Sent from the United Methodist Church in US
Bought the herb-roofed house and started ministry in Chung Cheong-do.

Missionary Robert Arthur Sharp
Got newly married to Alice H. Sharp in 1905
Began to spread the gospel in Gongju.

The next year, missionary Sharp attended the evangelism rally in Nonsan,
Escaped the rain in the funeral bier house
And was infected with typhoid fever and was called by God.

Missionary Frank E. C. Williams

군정軍政의 시작 1

칠흑 같은 어둠이 한반도를 드리웠네

어둠 속에서도 빛을 잉태한 복음福音의 씨앗은
교회敎會를 통해 문맹 퇴치 운동과
계몽 운동으로 발아發芽되었네

미국 감리교에서 파송된
윌리엄 맥길(William B. Mcgill) 선교사가
초가집 한 동을 구입하여 충청도에서 사역을 시작했네

로버트 아서 샤프(Robert Arthur Sharp) 선교사는
1905년, 엘리스 샤프(Alice H. Sharp)와 결혼한 후
공주에서 복음을 전하기 시작했네

이듬 해 논산에 전도 집회를 다녀오던 샤프 선교사는
비를 피하기 위해 들어간 상여집에서
장티푸스에 감염되어 하나님의 부름을 받았네

샤프 선교사의 후임으로 부임한

Was succeeded missionary Sharp.

He devoted himself to educating Koreans.
With the Korean name of Woo Ri-am
Establishing a school Young Myung School in 1906.

Patriotic martyr Yu Kwan-soon, Yoon Chang-suk and Cho Byung-ok
Were graduated from the Young Myung school.
This school became a mission center in Chungcheong area.
It was the epicenter of the independence movement.

George A. Williams was born in Incheon in 1907,
The eldest son of Missionary Frank William.

In 1910 when the Korea-Japan Annexation Treaty was signed,

Missionary Woo Ri-am wished for the liberation of Korea
Changed his son's name from George William to Korean name
Woo Kwang-bok.

In 1909, his daughter Olive was born.
And in 1919, she died of endemic disease at her age of 10.
He sent his son George William (Woo Kwang-bok) to his father in US.

프랭크 윌리엄(Frank E. C. Williams) 선교사

우리암禹利岩이라는 한국 명으로 사역한 그는
1906년, 영명 학교永明學校를 설립하여
한국인의 교육에 열정을 쏟았네

유관순柳寬順열사와 윤창석尹昌錫, 조병옥趙炳玉 등을
배출한 영명 학교는 충청 지역의 선교 중심지이며
독립 운동의 진앙지였네

1907년, 프랭크 윌리엄 선교사의 장남
조지 윌리엄(George A. Williams)이 인천에서 태어났네

1910년, 한일병합조약韓日倂合條約이 체결되자

대한민국의 광복光復을 소망하고
아들 조지 윌리엄의 한국식 이름을
우광복禹光復으로 작명한 우리암禹利岩 선교사

1909년 태어난 딸 올리브(Olive)가
10세의 어린 나이에 풍토병으로 사망하자
아들 조지 윌리엄〔禹光復〕을 아버지가 있는 미국으로 보냈네

In 1940, when the Pacific War finally was on its peak,
The Japanese closed the Young Myung School
And expelled the missionary Frank William (Woo Ri-am) from Korea.

George William (Woo Kwang-bok) graduated from
The Denver School of Medicine in Colorado State,
Participated in the Pacific War as naval surgeon.

1940년, 태평양 전쟁이 막바지에 이르자
영명학교永明學校를 폐쇄한 일본은
프랭크 윌리엄〔禹利岩〕 선교사를 조선에서 추방했네

콜로라도 주 덴버 의대를 졸업한 조지 윌리엄〔禹光復〕은
태평양 전쟁에 해군 군의관으로 참전參戰했네

The Beginning of Military Government 2

There were no Korean-speaking soldiers among the 10,000 soldiers in the 24th Corps of the US Army.

Lieutenant Colonel George William of the Navy
Belonged to the 7th Fleet which escorted 24th Corps
Went on the deck to report on Incheon landing.

Deck chief Colonel Hartman spoke in Italian, French and English
Meanwhile three Koreans were speaking each in Korean, Chinese and Japanese.

"These people are activists for independence who fought against Japan,
They came here to express their respect" interpreted lieutenant William.
And the colonel Hartman asked with pleasure "How come you understand Korean so well?"

"There's a red brick house with the black roof over the hill, I was born there"
Lieutenant William answered.

군정軍政의 시작 2

하지(John Reed Hodge) 장군이 지휘한 미 24군단
1만 명의 군사 가운데 한국어에 능통한 병사가 없었네

24군단을 호위하던 7함대 소속
해군 군의관 조지 윌리엄〔禹光復〕 중령은
상륙(인천) 보고를 위해 갑판에 올라갔네

갑판 책임자 하트먼 대령은 이탈리아어, 프랑스어, 영어로
한국인 3명은 중국어, 일어, 한국어로 제각기 말하고 있었네

"이 사람들은 일본과 싸운 독립 운동가들이며, 하지 중장에게
 존경을 표하고 싶어 찾아왔다."는 윌리엄 중령의 통역에
"어떻게 한국어를 그리 잘 아는가?"
하트먼 대령이 반색하며 반문했네

"저기 언덕 위에 보이는 검은 지붕의 붉은 벽돌집이
 내가 태어난 곳"이라고 윌리엄 중령이 대답했네

하트먼 대령의 소개로 윌리엄 중령은

With the introduction of Colonel Hartman, he was specially hired as an interpreter for Lieutenant general John Reed Hodge, commander of the US Army on September 8, 1945.

On September 8, 1945 lieutenant general Hodge landed on Wolmi-do Islet And advanced to Seoul, and received the surrender document from Abe Nobuyuki, Governor of Choseon on September 9, 1945.
Lieutenant general Hodge appointed major general Archibold V. Arnold as the military government minister of South Korea on September 12, 1945.

The first thing for US soldiers was to find out any Korean who could speak English.

Lieutenant general Hodge requested to lieutenant colonel George William, Who had good knowledge in Korean circumstances, to recommend 50 Koreans who were fluent in English to lead Korea in collaboration with the US Military Government.

Lieutenant colonel William consulted with his mother and delivered
The list of 50 selected Koreans.

Later, William's mother taught students in Ewha Women's University
And his father, missionary William (Woo Ri-am), was dedicated as an advisor to lieutenant general Hodge in agricultural area.

미 육군 사령관 하지 중장의
통역관으로 특채되었네

월미도에 상륙한 후(1945. 09. 08.) 서울로 진격
아베 노부유키 조선 총독으로부터
항복 문서를 접수한(1945. 09. 09.) 하지 중장은
남한의 군정장관(軍政長官)으로
아놀드(Archibold V. Arnold) 소장을 임명했네(1945. 09. 12.)

서울에 진주한 미군이 가장 먼저 한 일은
영어를 할 줄 아는 한국인을 찾는 일이었네

한국 사정에 밝은 조지 윌리엄 중령에게
하지 장군은 미 군정과 협력하며 한국을 이끌어 갈
영어에 능통한 인재 50명의 추천을 의뢰했네

윌리엄 중령은 어머니와 상의하여 선정한
한국인 명단 50명을 하지 장군에게 전달했네

그 후 윌리엄 중령의 어머니는
이화 여자 대학교에서 학생을 가르쳤고
아버지 윌리엄〔禹利岩〕 선교사는
하지 장군의 농업 고문으로 헌신했네

At 1 pm on the 10th of September
'Korean VIP invitation meeting' was held at Chosun Hotel.

Most of them studied in the US or Europe and Christians;
50 people including Lee Hun-gu, O Jung-soo and Cho Byung-ok
Started to work at the US Military Government office from the next day.

Bening Berehrhof was sent as political advisor to Hodge from the State Department.
He reported the first report to his home country on the 15th of September in a week of his arrival at Korea."

"South Korea is like a powder keg that will explode at once
If just fires a spark at one point.
Of the Cairo Declaration (which first unveiled Korea's independence)
The terminology" in due course" was known in Korea as saying "within a few days" or "soonest".
Therefore, Koreans didn't understand and are very much disappointed
The reason why there is no immediate and perfect independence.
Only one of the most encouraging elements in the political situation here is;
That there are hundreds of senior educated class conservatives in Seoul.

Most of them have a career in pro-Japanese cooperated with Japan
However this labeling will eventually disappear.
They are looking forward to returning of the Provisional Government.

9월 10일 오후 1시, 조선 호텔에서는
'조선인 유지 초청 간담회' 가 열렸네

대부분 유럽과 미국 유학생 출신이며 크리스찬들인
이훈구李勳求, 오정수, 조병옥 등 한국인 50명은
다음 날부터 미 군정 사무실로 출근했네

국무부에서 하지의 정치 고문으로 파견한 베닝 베렐호프는
한국에 온 지 일주일만에 첫 보고서를
본국에 보냈네(1945. 09. 15.)

"남한은 한 점의 불꽃만 튀겨도
곧 폭발하고 말 화약통과 같습니다.
(한국의 독립을 처음 밝힌) 카이로 선언의
'적절한 절차를 걸쳐(indue course)' 라는 말이
한국에서는 처음부터 '수일 내에' 또는
'빨리빨리' 라는 뜻으로 알려졌습니다.
따라서 한국인들은 미군이 도착한 후
즉각 완전한 독립이 주어지지 않는 이유를
이해하지 못하고 있으며 대단히 실망하고 있습니다.
이 곳의 정치 상황에서 가장 고무적인 단 하나의 요소는
서울의 나이 많고 교육받은 계층에
수백 명의 보수파가 있다는 사실입니다.

We can’t say it’s a majority of Koreans
But perhaps it’s the biggest one as a single group.”

The US Military Government was searching for cooperative Korean political forces,
Paid attention on the Democratic Party of Korea which started its activities earnestly since the US military arrived at Korea.

On the 11th of September, Colonel Cecilis Nist, the US intelligence agency chief, Had a meeting with Korea Democratic Party leaders such persons as Seo Sang-il, Seol Eui-ik and Kim Yong-moo etc.

He judged that “These persons were the prominent and respected businessmen and leaders.
The Korea Democratic Party is the most representative party of the entire Korean people, All of the members were judged to be capable and reputable conservatives.”

The US Army Intelligence Report for about 10 days after the US military arrival was Most of the quoted Korean information providers were those who had relations with the Korea Democratic Party.

The US military intelligence logbook on September 13 wrote as follows:
“Thus far, all information providers are in Chongqing China,
When the Korean Provisional Government, previously led by Rhee Syng-man, returns home,

이들의 대부분은 일제에 협력한 친일의 경력을 갖고 있지만
이 같은 낙인은 결국 사라질 것입니다.
이들은 임정臨政의 귀환을 고대하고 있으며
한국인의 다수라고 할 수는 없지만
아마도 단일 그룹에서는 최대일 것입니다."

협력적인 한국인 정치 세력을 물색하고 있던 미 군정은
미군 진주와 함께 본격적으로 활동을 개시한
한국민주당(한민당)을 주목했네

9월 11일, 미군 정보 기관 책임자인 세실 니스트 대령은
서상일, 설의식, 김용무 등 한민당 관계자들과 면담을 한 후

"이들은 저명하고 존경받는 실업인들과 지도자들로
한민당은 전체 한국인을 가장 잘 대표하는 정당이며
구성원들 모두 능력 있고 평판 좋은 보수주의자"
라고 판단했네

미군이 진주한 후, 약 10일 동안 미군 정보 보고서에
인용되고 있는 한국인 정보 제공자들의 대부분은
이들 한민당 관계자들이었네

9월 13일 자, 미군 정보일지는 이렇게 적고 있네

Will be great help to stabilize the political situation.
Most Koreans worship Rhee Syng-man as the Sun Wen of Korea.

Colonel William, who was appointed political advisor to the Arnold Marshal,
Previously interpreter for lieutenant general Hodge travelled to get information from the citizens in the cities such as Daejeon, Gwangju, Daegu and Busan, etc.

A comprehensive report of Benign Barelhoff's South Korean situation was:

It is reported on the 29th of September “South Korea's political forces are divided into two groups;
The Democratic conservatives and the Communist radical forces.
The conservative group, centered on the Korea Democratic Party, wants
The western democracy wishes the return of Rhee Syng-man and Provisional Government.
The political opportunists lead by pro-communist Yeo Wun-hyung
Wish to be under Soviet influence. They are ahead of conservatives
In terms of organization and propaganda”

"지금까지 모든 정보 제공자들은 충칭重慶에 있으며
 이전에 이승만이 이끌었던 한국 임시 정부가 돌아온다면
 정치 정세 안정에 큰 도움이 될 것이다. 대다수 한국인은
 이승만을 한국의 쑨원孫文으로 추앙하고 있다."

하지 장군의 통역관에서
아놀드 군정장관의 정치 고문으로 임명된 윌리엄 중령은
대전, 광주, 대구, 부산 등을 돌아다니며
민심의 동향을 파악했네

베닝 베렐호프의 남한 정세에 관해 포괄적인 보고서는

"남한의 정치 세력은 민주주의적 보수 세력과
 공산주의적 급진 세력으로 양분되어 있다.
 한민당을 중심으로 하는 보수 그룹은
 서구 민주주의를 원하고
 이승만과 임정의 환국을 희망하고 있다.
 용공적 성향의 정치적 기회주의자 여운형이 이끌고 있는
 급진파는 소련의 영향을 받고 있는 것 같다.
 그들은 보수파에 비해 조직과 선전 활동면에서 앞서 있다."
라 기록하고 있네(1945. 09. 29.)

The Beginning of Military Government 3

With the declaration of war against Japan on August 9, 1945
The Soviet army entered North Korea and occupied Pyongyang on August 26th.

General I. M. Chistiakov, commander of the Soviet Union's 25th Army,
Was going to establish a Soviet-friendly political system in North Korea
And ordered the dissolution of registration system of all political parties
All organizations and armed forces as well,
And guided all the activities and censored publications
Through Romanenko, A.A. of Political Command.The Soviet army that occupied North Korea
Disconnected the railway Kyungwon Line on the 24th of August, And the next day the Gyeongeui Line on the 25th of August.
And then they put security forces on the 38 parallel, and started to control the traffics.

The parallel line 38 was created to disarm the Japanese army
But it was started to turn into a political division line.

According to the 'Article 1 of the Guidelines for the Establishment of People's Government' Which was announced by the Soviet military commander on September 09, 1945

군정軍政의 시작 3

대일 선전 포고(1945. 08. 09.)와 함께
북한에 들어온 소련군은 8월 26일, 평양을 점령했네

소련군 제25군 사령관 치스차코프(I. M. Chistiakov) 대장은
북한 지역에 우호적인 정치 체제 수립을 위하여
모든 정당과 단체의 등록제, 무장 부대의 해산을 명령하고
로마넨코(Romanenko, A. A.) 정치 사령부를 통해
제반 활동을 지도하며 출판물에 대한 검열을 실시했네

북한을 점령한 소련군은
남북을 연결하는 경원선 철도를(1945. 08. 24.)
그 다음날에는 경의선 철도를 차단한 후에
38선에 경비부대를 배치하여 통행의 통제를 시작했네

일본군의 무장 해제를 위해 만들어진 38선이
정치적 분단선으로 변질되기 시작했네

소련군 사령부가 발표한(1945. 09. 14.)
「인민정부수립요강」 1조에 의하면

“It was declared that the Soviet Union will establish a government of labors and farmers And propose to the four countries, the Soviet Union, the United States, Great Britain and China.

In order to execute this, they tried to establish a communist state in North Korea like the Soviet Union by carrying out land reform, purging pro-Japanese persons and put the individual managements under their special supervision.

South Korea was started to be governed by major general Arnold of the US military, North Korea was started to be governed by major general Romanenko of the Soviet military from September 20, 1945.

Park Hun-young who organized Kyung Sung Com Group and guided it Fled to Gwangju when the Japanese police narrowed to arrest him.
He worked at Bae Kun-dong brick factory under nickname of Kim Sung-sik. He hurriedly came to Seoul on August 19, 1945 when liberation was realized.

Park Hun-young was working hard to rebuild the Communist Party together with Kim Sam-yong and Lee Hyun-sang when they saw the Jangan Group formed Communist Party on August 16, 1945, Park Hun-young was against this and he organized the Central Committee of the Communist Party of Korea and became responsible secretary in the joint meeting of Jangan Group and Reconstruction Group on September 3, 1945.

"소비에트 연방은 끝끝내 노동자, 농민 정권의 수립을
 소련, 미국, 영국, 중국 4국에 제안할 것"을 명시하고 있네

이를 위해 토지 개혁을 실시하고, 친일파를 숙청하고
개인의 경영을 특별한 감시 아래 둠으로써
소련과 같은 공산주의 체제의 국가를 북한에 세우려 했네

남한南韓은 아놀드 소장에 의한 미국의 군정 통치가 **「註釋*11」**
북한北韓은 로마넨코 소장에 의한
소련의 군정 통치가 시작됐네(1945. 09. 20.) **「註釋*12」**

경성콤 그룹을 조직하여 지도하던 중
일본 경찰의 눈을 피해 김성식이라는 이름으로
광주 백운동 벽돌 공장에 은신하고 있던 박헌영朴憲永은
해방이 되자 서둘러 서울로 올라왔네(1945. 08. 19.)

장안파 공산당이 결성되자(1945. 08. 16.)
이에 대항하여 김삼룡金三龍, 이현상李鉉相 등과 함께
공산당의 재건을 위해 열심히 뛰던 박헌영은
장안파와 재건파의 연석 회의를 통해(1945. 09. 03.)
조선공산당 중앙 기구를 구성하고 책임비서가 되었네
「註釋*13」

The 88th Reconnaissance Brigade was waiting to fight against Japanese Emperor, All operation plans were canceled when Soviet Union declared war against Japan on August 9, 1945.

The Soviet Union decided to send 80 Kim Il-sung troops from 88 Reconnaissance Brigade who did not participate in the war against Japan to the Soviet military border guard command stationed in North Korea.

Before sending 88 Brigades to North Korea
Stalin called Kim Il-sung to Moscow early September, And decided after interview to appoint Kim as North Korea's top leader candidate.

Captain Kim Il-sung of the Soviet Army drove 80 soldiers
Landed at Wonsan port on the 19th of September
Under the protection of the Soviet Army.

"The North Korean leader must be a Communist Party member
But the North Korean leader Park Hun-young was in Seoul.
And there was no reliable Communist Party member in North Korea."

This was a report from the Soviet 25th Army Headquarter stationed in Pyongyang.

Ahead of the meeting of responsible and enthusiastic persons of the five North Korean provinces,

일제日帝와의 전투를 위해 대기하고 있던
88정찰여단은 소련이 대일 선전 포고를 한 후(1945. 08. 09.)
모든 작전 계획作戰計劃이 취소되었네

소련은 대일전對日戰에 참전하지 못한
88정찰여단의 김일성 부대 80명을
북한 주둔 소련군 위수 사령부에 파견키로 결정했네

88여단을 북한에 파견하기 전
김일성을 모스크바로 불러 독대한 스탈린은(9월 초)
북한의 최고 지도자 후보로 김일성金日成을 낙점落點했네

소련군 대위 김일성은 소련군의 비호 아래
대원 80명을 이끌고 원산항에 상륙했네(1945. 09. 19.)

"북조선의 지도자는 공산당원이 되어야 하는데
조선공산당 지도자 박헌영은 서울에 있고
북조선에는 믿을 만한 공산당원이 없다."
는 평양 주둔 소련군 제25군 사령부의 보고가 있었네

조선공산당 북부 5도당 책임자 및 열성자 회의를 앞두고
개성 북방의 소련군 38경비 사령부에서 진행된
김일성과 박헌영의 제1차 비밀 회동에는(10. 08.~10. 09.)

Kim Il-sung and Park Hun-young's first secret meeting was held on October 8-9 at the 38 Security Command of Soviet Army in Kaesong, North Korea.

The participants were major general Romenenko, Soviet Army Political Commander, Joo Young-ha, Chang Soon-myung, Lee Ju-yeon and Park Jung-ae from Kim Il-sung side, and Kwon Oh-jik, Lee In-dong and Heo Seong-taek from Park Hun young side.

The agenda of the meeting was 'Establishment of the North Korean branch of the Communist Party of Korea and the place where to position the Headquarter of Communist Party of Korea'.

Afterwards, the meeting of responsible and enthusiastic persons of the five North Korean provinces was held behind closed doors in Pyongyang during $10^{th} \sim 13^{th}$ of October.

"Kim Il-sung who was supported by Soviet Army insisted that
Separate northern area and make it communist first and
Using it as base, make the southern area communist next.
In order for this plan to be effectively executed,The communist party should be organized in North Korea independently."

Domestic communists who followed Park Hun-young
Strongly opposed to the claim of Kim Il-sung on the basis of the principle of the Party To have one party in one country based on the Communist

소련군 정치사령관 로마넨코 소장과
김일성 측의 주영하, 장순명, 이주연, 박정애
박헌영 측의 권오직, 이인동, 허성택 등이 참석했네

회동의 의제는 '조선공산당 북조선 분국 창설 문제' 와
'조선공산당 중앙당의 위치를 어디에 두느냐?' 였네

조선공산당 '북부 5도당 책임자 및 열성자 대회' 가
평양에서 비공개로 개최됐네(10. 10.~10. 13)

소련군의 지원을 받고 있던 김일성은

"북한 지역을 분리하여 먼저 공산화하고
 공산화된 북한을 기지로 삼아 남한까지 공산화해야 한다.
 이 계획을 효과적으로 진전시키기 위해서는
 북한에 독자적 공산당이 조직되어야 한다."
고 주장했네

박헌영을 추종하는 국내파 공산주의자들이
공산당의 1국 1당 조직 원칙을 근거로
김일성의 주장을 완강히 반대하자
우선 북한에 조선공산당 북조선 분국을 설치하고
임시로 제1비서에 김용범을 선출했네(1945. 10. 13.)

Party's Principle.

Kim Il-sung established the subdivision of North Korean Communist Party and it temporarily elected Kim Yong-bum as the first secretary on the 13th of October.

Soviet army captain Kim Il-sung who was 33-year-old
Appeared to the public decorated as nation's hero in "The People's Rally of Welcome of Victorious Returning Home of General Kim Il-sung" by the guide of the Soviet Political Commander, Romanenko held in Pyongyang City on the 14th of October.

At the third meeting of the Executive Committee of the Communist Party of North Korea branch was held on the 17th of December, the Communist Party organization bureau and
Changed the 1st secretary from Kim Yong-bum to Kim Il-sung.

The first task of the Soviet military government was
How to set the relationship between the nationalist Cho Man-sik and
Kim Il-sung whom they are training as the leader.

A command arrived from Moscow:
"Do not raise the communist party member in front of the regime
But let the nationalist or democrat be raised first"

Cho Man-sik, chairman of the People's Committee of the Pyongnam province,

33살의 소련군 대위 김일성金日成은
소련군 정치 사령관 로마넨코 소장에 의해
〈김일성 장군 개선 환영 군중 대회〉에서(1945. 10. 14.)
민족의 영웅으로 각색되어 대중 앞에 나타났네

조선공산당 북조선 분국
제3차 집행 위원회 회의에서(1945. 12. 17.)
북조선공산당 조직국은
제1비서를 김용범에서 김일성으로 변경했네

소련 군정청의 첫 과제는
민족주의자 조만식曺晩植과
자신들이 지도자로 양성 중인 김일성과의 관계 설정이었네

모스크바로부터

"공산당원을 정권의 전면에 부상시키지 말고
 민족주의자나 민주주의자를 먼저 내세워라."
는 지령이 내려왔네

평남인민위원회 위원장 조만식과 소련 군정은
모스크바 삼상 회의의 결과가 나오기 전부터
수 차례 만나 북조선의 정치 현안에 대해 논의했네

And Soviet military government had several times of meeting to discuss Political issues in North Korea before the outcome of result in the Moscow three foreign ministers meeting.

Cho Man-sik was passive, stating that it will be a paralyzed on one side party in case
The party is composed only with North Korean party, to the recommendation of Soviet Military Government to establish the national camp. However he made his mind after hearing Kim Il-sung's saying: "If you establish the party I will also be a member I will take a role of bridge between you and the Soviet Military Government."

Cho Man-sik rejected when he was recommended to be the chairman of the North Korean People's Political Commission, became the Party leader of the Democratic Party of Korea on the 3rd of November by establishing this party.

Rev. Han Kyung-jik and Rev. Yoon Ha-young were doing ministry in the churches in Sinuiju, Pyongbuk Province established Christian Social Democratic Party in September.

The Soviet army was embarrassed to see the party was expanding
Its power all of a sudden and Soviet Army began to oppress the Christian Social Democratic Party Composed mostly by Christians.

At the organization meeting of the Yongampo district party held on the

민족 진영의 정당 창당을 권하는 소련 군정의 권유에
북조선만의 반신불수 정당이라며 소극적이던 조만식은
"창당하면 입당하여 소련 군정과의 가교 역할을 하겠다."
는 김일성의 말을 듣고 창당을 결심했네

북조선인민정치위원회 위원장 추대를 거절한 조만식은
조선민주당을 창당하여 당수가 되었네(1945. 11. 03.) 「註釋*14」

평안북도 신의주에서 목회를 하고 있던
한경직韓景職 목사와 윤하영尹河英 목사는
기독교사회민주당을 창당했네(1945. 09.) 「註釋*15」

기독교인들이 중심이 된
기독교사회민주당 당세가 급격히 확산되자
당황한 소련군이 탄압하기 시작했네

용암포에서 개최된 지구당 조직 대회장에(1945. 11. 16.)
수백 명의 공산당원들이 난입亂入하여
위원장 장원봉張元鳳과 간부를 구타하고 살해하자
의분義憤한 신의주 학생들이 일어났네

"소련군은 물러가라."
"공산당을 몰아내자."

16th of November, hundreds of Communists members broke into the place and murdered by beating

The committee chairman Jang Won-bong and the executive officers.

The Sinuiju students were burn in righteous indignation rose up.

The students shout out the slogans "Soviets go home!"
"Let's drive out the Communist Party."
"Let's retake the freedom of the academy"
3,500 middle school students started marching in the city.

Soviet military was surprised and declared martial law.
They started ruthless suppression by mobilizing tanks and fighter planes.

We have forgotten the history and history has forgotten the Sinuiju Students' uprising who have been brutally suppressed
And was resulted numerous victims (23 killed, 700 injured).

"학원의 자유를 쟁취하자."
는 구호를 외치며
중등학생 3,500여 명의 시가 행진이 시작됐네

놀란 소련군은 계엄령을 선포하고
전차와 비행기까지 동원, 무자비한 진압을 시작했네

수많은 희생자(피살자 23명, 부상자 700여 명)를 내고
잔인하게 진압된 신의주 학생 의거를 「註釋*16」
우리는 잊고 있네, 역사가 잊고 있네

The Beginning of Military Government 4

Rhee Syng-man's status was stateless asylum-seeker for 34 years
And he needed permission from the US Department of State to return home.

From the end of August he tried in every way to get a travel certificate
To go to Korea but it was not easy to solve as he was labeled as an "Anti-American person."

He was hated by Dean Gooderham Acheson (1893～1971), the Deputy Secretary of State of US as Rhee Syng-man was anti-communist and bothered the State of Department for years.

George W. William (Woo Gwang-bok), a military adviser who travelled to conduct a public opinion poll throughout South Korea to take a role of bridge between the US Military Government and
South Koreans, sent a report to General Hodge. He mentioned in his report that South Korean people want Rhee Syng-man to be repatriated calling him "Our President".

In mid-October, the US State Department issued an order to the Army Commander of the State Department for the Pacific;

군정軍政의 시작 4

34년째 무국적無國籍 망명자亡命者 신분이였던
이승만의 귀국은 미 국무부의 허가가 필요했네

8월 하순부터 한국행 여행 증명서 발급을 위해
백방으로 뛰었지만 '반미적反美的 인사' 로 낙인찍힌
이승만의 귀국길은 쉽게 열리지 않았네

반공주의자로 그 동안 미 국무부를 괴롭힌 이승만을
딘 애치슨(Dean Gooderham Acheson, 1893~1971) 국무차관이
싫어했기 때문이었네

미 군정과 한국인의 가교 역할을 하기 위해
남한 전역을 돌며 여론 조사를 한
조지 윌리엄〔禹光復〕 군정 고문은
한국인들이 이승만을 '우리 대통령' 이라 부르며
귀국을 원하고 있다고 여러 차례 하지 장군에게 보고했네

10월 중순, 국무성이 태평양 방면 육군 총사령부에 보낸 훈령은

“The United States Pacific Army General Command should review the Korea policy which has assumed the process of independence of Korea through two steps;
The Soviet Union and the United States civilian administration govern the postwar Korea
And then execute it by the International Trusteeship of the Soviet Union, USA, United Kingdom and China.

US State Department, which has blocked the repatriation of Rhee Syng-man
On account of his being “Anti-American person”, reluctantly accepted the strong request of general Hodge who insisted Rhee Syng-man’s returning home is required for the stability of the country.

He wanted to go back home as soon as possible.

Rhee Syng-man departed New York on the 4th of October and arrived at Tokyo via Hawaii and Guam. In Tokyo he had a meeting with MacArthur on the 12th of October.
He arrived at Gimpo Airport on the 16th of October together with general Hodge who went to Tokyo to meet him by US military plane.

At 8:30 pm on that evening, he gave a speech through radio (Seoul Central Broadcasting Station)
“Follow me, if you stand together, you’ll live and if you scatter, you’ll die.”

"소련과 미국의 민간 행정부가 전후 조선을 지배하고
소련, 미국, 영국, 중국의 국제 신탁 통치가 실시되는
두 단계를 거쳐 조선을 독립시키는 과정을 상정한 조선
정책을 미국 태평양 방면 육군 총사령부가 검토해야 한다."
는 내용이었네

'반미적反美的 인사' 이승만의 귀국길을 막던 미 국무부는
하지 장군이 정국의 안정을 위해 이승만의 귀국을
강력히 요청하자 마지 못해 허락했네

하루라도 빨리 고국으로 돌아가고 싶었네

뉴욕을 떠난(1945. 10. 04.) 이승만은 하와이 괌을 거쳐
도쿄東京에서(1945. 10. 12.) 맥아더와 회동한 후
도쿄까지 마중 나온 하지 장군과 함께
미 군용기편으로 김포 공항에 도착했네(1945. 10. 16.)

이 날 저녁 8시 30분, 그는 라디오(서울 중앙 방송국)를 통해
"나를 따르시오, 뭉치면 살고 흩어지면 죽습니다."
라는 연설로 국민들의 심금을 울렸네

His speech touched the people's heart.

The Adjustment Committee of the US Department of State, the US Army, US Navy and the Far East Subcommittee was going to draft a report.
In the process of drafting a report, it insisted that the Soviet and US military
Occupation of postwar Korea should be replaced by the international trusteeship as soon as possible. And it insisted that the International political talks should be opened soon in order to conduct the international trusteeship on October 20, 1945.

The Stars and Stripes published by the US Army Headquarters reported on October 20, 1945
That John Carter Vincent, US State Department Far East Director reported at the Council on Foreign Relations in New York:
"Choseon has no capability to govern itself and should be governed under the international trusteeship".

Kim Gu (nickname Baekbum) requested to the Chief of the Republic of China, Jiang Jieshi of his return to Korea after getting an approval from US for the Provisional Government as, at least, Korea's transitional regime.
However, the US Military Government refused to accept it under the policy of no any previous government can't be recognized.

미 국무성은 국무성, 육군성, 해군성 조정위원회
극동소위원회가 입안한 보고서에서

전후戰後 조선에 대한 소련과 미국의 군사 점령이
하루 빨리 국제 신탁 통치로 대체되어야 하며
국제 신탁 통치를 실시하기 위한 국제 정치 회담이
하루 속히 열려야 한다고 주장했네(1945. 10. 20.)

미국 육군 사령부가 펴내는 '성조기(The Stars and Stripes)' 는
국무성 극동국장 존 빈센트(John Carter Vincent)가
뉴욕에 있는 대외관계협의회(Council on Foreign Relations)에서
"조선은 자치 능력이 없어 국제 신탁 통치를 실시해야 할 것"
이라고 말했음을 보도했네(1945. 10. 20.)

백범白凡 김구金九는 중화민국의 장제스에게
최소한 임시 정부를 한국의 과도 정권으로 미국이 묵인한 후에
귀국할 수 있도록 부탁했으나 기존에 있던 어떤 정부도
그 실체를 인정할 수 없다며 미 군정은 거절했네

미 군정이 임시 정부의 실체를 인정하지 아니하자
일본이 항복한 지 3개월 8일 만에
충칭重慶에서 상하이上海에 도착한 후 18일만에
이승만이 귀국한 지 1개월 17일이 지나

As the US military government didn't recognize the reality of the Provisional Government,
Kim Gu could return to Korea as only personal status on the 23rd of November
By a freight plane provided by the US in three months and eight days after Japan's surrender 18 days after his arrival at Shanghai from Chongqing
After 1 month and 17 days after the return of Rhee Syng-man.

On the day of his repatriation, Kim Gu issued a brief statement:
"We brought the government but our government still can't have relations with foreign countries
So long as the military government exists.
We came back individually."

김구는 개인 자격으로 미국이 제공한
미군 수송기에 탑승하여 귀국(1945. 11. 23.)할 수 있었네

김구는 귀국한 날, 기자 회견을 통해

"우리는 정부를 가져왔지만 군정이 있는 한
우리 정부는 아직 외국과의 관계를 갖지 못한다.
우리는 개인 자격으로 들어왔다."
는 짤막한 내용의 성명을 발표했네

Song Jin-woo's (pen name Koha) Assassination

He was offered to participate in the Founding Committee of the Nation
However, Song Jin-woo rejected this recommendation
He waited for Japanese Chosen Governor to transfer the government to the Allied military.

When the news of US Military advancement in the South of 38 parallel was delivered
People organized the 'Welcoming Preparatory Committee for the Provisional Government and Allied Forces' on the 1st of September. And people insisted to give a priority to the Provisional Government.

A part of leftist powers of the Provisional Government Preparatory Committee declared the People's Republic.

Rightist leaders who were in the domestic who supported the Provisional Government of the Republic of Korea in Chongqing, China established the Preparations for the National Convention at the Dong-A Daily Newspaper Company on the 7th of September to collect the people's general opinion.
The Preparatory Committee of National Convention, the Goryeo Democratic Party, the Chosen Nationalist Party and the Korean Nationalist Party created the Korean Democratic Party at the Chondogyo Memorial Hall in Seoul on the 16th of September.

고하 송진우의 암살

건국준비위원회의 참여를 제의받았으나
거절한 고하古下 송진우宋鎭禹는
조선 총독부가 연합군에게 정권을 인도하기를 기다렸네

38선 이남에 대한 미군의 진주가 알려지자
'임시 정부 및 연합군 환영 준비위원회' 를
조직하고(1945. 09. 01.)
임정 봉대론臨政奉戴論을 주장했네 「註釋*17」

건준의 일부 좌익 세력이
인민공화국人民共和國을 선포했네

국내에 있는 우익 지도자들은
충칭重慶에 있는 대한민국 임시 정부를 지지하는
국민의 총의를 한데 모으기 위한
국민대회준비회를 동아일보사에서 결성했네(1945. 09. 07.)

국민대회준비회, 고려민주당, 조선민족당, 한국국민당 등은
서울 천도교 기념관에서 한국민주당을 창당했네(1945. 09. 16.)

Chang Duk-soo (pen name Seolsan) declared to beat the People's Republic of Korea while Expressing the absolute support of the Chongqing Provisional Government at the inauguration statement of the Korean Democratic Party.

Song Jin-woo (pen name Koha) was recommended as the chief secretary of the party.

The Central Council for Independence Promotion recommended Rhee Syng-man as chairman, which was formed with the aim of sole political organization in South Korea comprising 200 participants including leftists and rightists at the Chosun Hotel on the 23rd of October.

Rhee Syng-man, chairman of the Central Council for Independence Promotion Attacked Communism vigorously through the radio broadcasting on the 21th November,
The general Hodge was surprised and shocked.

The leftists Yeo Wun-hyung, the People's Party and the Korean Communist Party members Got out of the pre-negotiation meeting to organize Central Council for Independence Promotion On the 28th November on account of the Korea Democratic Party (Song Jin-woo line) members Are 5 among the total 7 examination members.

The Provisional Government was not willing to accept the Rhee Syng-man's plan to participate first in the Central Council for Independence

설산雪山 장덕수張德秀는 한민당 창당 발기문에서
조선인민공화국 타도와 충칭 임시 정부의 절대 지지를 밝혔네

수석 총무에 고하古下 송진우宋鎭禹를 추대했네

조선 호텔에서 각 정당 대표 200명이 참석하여
좌, 우익을 망라한
남한 내 유일한 정치 단체를 목적으로 결성된
독립촉성중앙협의회(독촉)는
회장에 이승만을 추대했네(1945. 10. 23.) 「註釋*18」

독립촉성중앙협의회 회장 이승만이 라디오 방송을 통해
공산주의를 격렬하게 공격하자(1945. 11. 21.) 「註釋*19」
하지 장군은 깜짝 놀랐네, 큰 충격을 받았네

독촉의 중앙 위원회 구성을 위한 사전 모임에서
전형 위원 7명 중 5명이 한민당(송진우 계열) 당원이라는 이유로
여운형과 인민당, 조선공산당 등의
좌파 세력은 이탈하였네(1945. 11. 28.)

임시 정부 또한 독촉에 참여한 후 임정을 해산한다는
이승만의 계획을 수락할 수 없어 독자적 조직화를 모색했네

Promotion, and then will dissolve the Provisional Government, and the Provisional Government members tried to organize another organization Themselves alone.

When the Dong-A daily newspaper was reissued on the 1st of December Song Jin-woo (nickname Koha) took the office as the 8th president of the company.

Three foreign ministers from US, England and Russia had a meeting at Moscow During 16th of December till 25th of December to deal with 7 postwar issues of the World War II.

Under the United Nations leadership, US submitted a regulation on the 16th of December to Govern Korea under the trusteeship of 4 nations; US, England, China and Soviet Union for 5 years (may extend for 5 years). Meanwhile, Soviet Union paid focused attention on the Japan matter.

With the concession of the United States to Soviet Union on the matter of Japan
On the 18th～19th, the Soviets accepted the US claim on the Chinese issue as they were able to participate in dealing the matter of occupying the Japanese Islands.

The United States wanted a US-friendly Korean government under the capitalism system (3 Nations of US, England and China) (Trusteeship first and establishment of government next).

동아일보가 복간되자(1945. 12. 01.)
8대 사장에 고하 송진우가 취임했네

제2차 세계 대전의 전후 문제 처리를 위한
7개의 의제를 협의하기 위해 미국, 영국, 소련 3국의 외상들이
모스크바에 모였네(1945. 12. 16～12. 25)

유엔 주도하에 한국에 대한 미국, 영국, 중국, 소련 4개 국의
5년(5년 연장 가능) 내 신탁 통치를 규정한
미국 안이 제출되었고(1945. 12. 16.)
소련은 일본 문제에 집중하고 있었네

미국의 양보로 일본 열도 점령에 참여할 수 있게 된
소련은 중국 문제에 대한 미국의 주장을 수락했네

미국은 자본주의 체제(미국, 영국, 중국 3국)에 의한
미국에게 우호적인 한국 정부를 원했고(선, 탁치/후, 정부 수립)
상대적으로 불리했던 소련은
조선인 참여를 보장한 후 소련에 우호적인
한국 정부를 수립하려고 했네(선, 임시 정부 수립/후, 후견)

한국에 관해 모스크바 삼상 회의는 「**註釋*20**」

And the Soviet Union, which was relatively unfavorable position, was trying to establish
A Soviet- friendly Korean government.(Establishing temporary government first and sponsor next).

With regard to the Korean matter, the three ministers' meeting was held in Moscow;

"To establish a Joint Committee participated by the United States and Soviet Union (hereinafter called as Joint Committee) to make an appropriate measures to help the Korean Provisional Government consisting of representatives of the US Army Command in South Korea and the Soviet Command in North Korea"

"The trusteeship agreement discussed and prepared by the Provisional Government, the political parties and social groups to govern the government by the four nations up to five years at most to be discussed by the four governments, and final decision is to be made by the US and Soviet governments.

The US and Soviet army commandments agreed each other "The emergency talks is to be held within two weeks"

"The decision was to establish the US and Soviet Joint Committee in Korea And they will discuss about the trusteeship for a certain period of time"

"한국의 임시 정부를 돕기 위한 적절한 방책을 만들기 위하여
남한의 미군 사령부와 북한의 소련 사령부의 대표로 구성된
미소공동위원회(공위)를 설립한다."

"임시 정부와 정당 사회 단체와 협의하여 마련된
최고 5개 년에 걸친 4개 국 탁치 협정안을
4개 국 정부가 심의하고, 미국과 소련 정부가 최종 결정한다."

"미군, 소련군 사령부의 긴급 회담을 2주 내로 개최한다."
고 합의했네

"한국에 미소공동위원회를 설치하고 「註釋*21」
일정 기간의 신탁 통치에 관해 협의한다." 「註釋*22」
는 결정이었네

12월 27일 자(26일 배포) 동아일보에 실린 외신 기사는
사실 관계가 부정확한 기사로
해방 정국에 엄청난 파장을 일으켰네

'소련은 신탁 통치 주장' 이란 기사는
태평양 성조기에 실린 기사를 합동 통신에서 받아
국내 신문들이 기사화한 내용이었네
(동아일보, 조선일보, 서울신문, 중앙신문, 조선신보 게재)

The Dong-A Daily Newspaper's article for overseas on the 27th of December (distributed on the 26th) provoked a big wave to the political atmosphere of liberation as this article was inaccurate one.

The article "The Soviet Union claimed trusteeship" was written by domestic newspapers Receiving the article from the Associated Press which acquired it from the Pacific Stars and Stripes (This article was published simultaneously on the newspapers such as Dong-A Ilbo,

Chosun Ilbo, The Seoul Shinmun, Joong Ang Shinmun, and Chosun Shinbo)

This was the Intentionally distorted newspaper articles for overseas Which was reported as it was without correction in relation with the result of the three foreign Ministers' meeting in Moscow.

This article took a definite role to change the liberation situation of people which was divided into pro and anti-liquidation of Japanese Imperialism into anti-Soviet and anti-communist ideological conflict through pro and anti-trusteeship.

Representatives of right-wing and mid-line political parties and social organizations gathered at the Gyunggyojang on the 27th of December except Rhee Syng-man who couldn't attend because he caught serious cold.

모스크바 삼상 회의 결과를
의도적으로 왜곡한 외신 기사를
가감 없이 그대로 보도한 신문 기사는

일제 청산 위한 민족과 반민족으로 나누던 해방 정국을
신탁 통치 반대와 찬성을 통해 반소, 반공의 이념 갈등으로
국면을 전환시키는 데 결정적인 역할을 했네

감기, 몸살 때문에 회의에 참석 못한 이승만을 제외한
우익과 중도 계열 정당 및 사회 단체의 대표들이
경교장에 모였네(1945. 12. 27.)

김구와 임시 정부는
신탁 통치 반대 국민 총동원 위원회를 조직하고
임시 정부 국무 위원회가 이를 지도하도록 함으로써
정국의 주도권을 장악하려고 했네

"신탁 통치 순응자는 반역자로 처단한다."
는 구호와 함께 전국적인 파업을 명령했네

미 군정 치하의 경찰을 비롯한 한인 관리들에게

Kim Gu and the Provisional Government organized the People's All-out Mobilization Committee against the Trusteeship and tried to take the leadership of the government By making the Provisional Government Council guided the Committee.

Under the motto of "The trusteeship supporters are to be punished as rebels." They ordered to enter into strike.

They prepared to issue the decree to the Korean officials including the police who are under the US Military Government to follow the order of the Provisional Government.

Song Jin-woo, who attended at the Gyunggyojang office meeting on the 29th of December,
Had a consultation with Arnold A. V, US military minister with regard to the trusteeship.

As the Provisional Government led the discussion to the direction to attempt to snatch
The US Military Government with the support of public opinion
But he decided that it is reckless attempt to do so and spoke let them cool down.

"I understand that all of your thoughts are caused by patriotism
However, we are the leaders of the nation and should not be frivolous.

임정의 명령을 따르라는 국자(포고령)를 준비했네

신탁 통치 문제로 아놀드(Arnold, A. V.) 미 군정장관과 면담한 후
경교장 회의에 참석한 송진우(1945. 12. 29.)는

임정이 여론을 몰아 미 군정을 접수하고
정권을 탈취하겠다는 방향으로 논의를 끌고 가자
무모한 시도라고 판단해 냉정을 촉구하는 발언을 했네

"여러분의 그런 생각 모두가
애국심에서 나온 것이란 것은 알고 있지만
나라를 이끄는 지도자들인 우리가 경박해서는 안 되지요.

여기 계신 여러분 중 누구라도
모스크바 3상 회의에서 결정된 의정서의 원본을
제대로 읽어본 분이 있습니까?

내가 알고 있기로는 미소공동위원회를 설치한 후에
한국의 정당, 사회 단체들과 협의해서
남북을 통일한 임시 정부를 세우고
5년 이내의 신탁 통치를 하는 것으로 되어 있습니다.

Did anyone of you here read the original protocols in due course?
That was decided at the three foreign ministers meeting in Moscow.

So far as I know, it is to establish a temporary government of unified Korea between North and South discussing with Korean political parties and social organizations after setting up the US and Soviet Joint Committee, and to conduct the trusteeship for 5 years.
If this is correct, there is no reason to object to it in extreme ways
As in five years we can build our unified independent government.

Even if we build government with our own strength,
We are under situation that it is currently under divided governing.

Under the circumstance of pending matters of post-war,

I think there is nothing we can do without having the super powers agreement

Trusteeship ruling is a five-year term but this can be changed to three years.There is no reason to oppose it nationally.
Of course, I myself also oppose the trusteeship.
Therefore let's be cold enough and let's have enough time
To consider the way how we will oppose to it".

Song Jin-woo's remarks called for a fierce resistance by the Provisional Government.

이것이 정확하다면 5년 후에는
통일된 우리의 독립 정부를 세울 수 있는 것을
극단적인 방법으로 반대할 이유가 없지 않습니까?

어차피 우리 힘으로 정부를 세운다고 해도
현재 분할 통치되고 있는 상황입니다.

강대국 간에 전후 처리 문제가
해결되지 않은 상태에서 그들의 합의 없이
우리 마음대로 할 수 있는 게 아니잖습니까?

신탁 통치가 5년이라고 하나 3년도 될 수 있는 것인데
이렇게 거국적으로 반대할 이유가 뭐 있습니까?
물론 나도 신탁 통치는 반대합니다.
반대 방법을 여유를 가지고
우리 모두 냉정하게 생각해 봅시다."

송진우의 발언은 임시 정부의 결렬한 저항을 불렀네

신탁 통치 반대를 제2의 독립 운동으로 생각한 이들에게
차분하고 냉정한 송진우의 발언은 신탁 통치 찬성으로 들렸네

Those who considered the opposition to trusteeship as the second independent movement,Song Jin-woo's calm and cool remarks sounded like in favor of the trusteeship.

Despite Kim Gu's discouraging to remain in the Gyunggyojang as it will be dangerous,
Song Jin-woo returned to his home in Wonseo-dong although Kim Gu dissuaded him.
He was attacked by the six attackers, Han Hyeon-woo and five others, and died at his home on the 30th of December.

Gain Kim Byung-ro selected two prominent righteous persons in Korea;
They were Yulgok Yiyi and Goha Song Jin-woo.

Widang Jung In-bo who compared Song Jin-woo to Admiral Yi Soon-sin
Inscribed sad lyrics on the epitaph of Song Jin-woo:

"The righteous persons are very rare to finish their lives as destined.They regard death as usual one
And go their way as they have to.

All the people are in sorrow;
The wives and children cry,
New Year's Eve at Mangwoo-ri cemetery
Only snow is falling!"

위험할 줄 모르니 경교장에 머물라는
김구의 만류에도 불구하고

원서동 자택으로 돌아간 송진우는
다음날 새벽 한현우韓賢宇 등 6명의 습격을 받고
자택에서 숨졌네(1945. 12. 30.) 「註釋*23」

가인街人 김병로金炳魯는 조선이 낳은 두 인물로
율곡栗谷 이이李耳와 고하 송진우를 꼽았네

송진우를 충무공 이순신에 비유했던 위당爲堂 정인보鄭寅普는
송진우의 비문에 서러운 노랫말을 새기었네

"의인은 예로부터
목숨대로 생을 마치는 일이 드물고
죽음을 예사로 여겨
갈 길을 돌아가는 듯하네

온 나라가 모두 슬퍼하고
처자는 소리내어 우는데
섣달 그믐 망우리에는
눈만 펄펄 내리는가."

Against Trusteeship

Policy of colonization was means of expanding the territory of imperialists was changed into the policy of exploiting the colonies.

Japanese imperialists subordinated small and weak countries under the pretext of protection treaty and made them semi-colonization, and they committed social and economic exploitation.

So-called mandatory rule or trusteeship was disguised one as non-colonization although
It was an actual colonial rule. It was a means of ruling the defeated country by the allies who won the war.

The mandatory rule exercised by the victorious country after the World War I
And the trusteeship system exercised by the United Nations after the World War II
To promote the autonomy and independence of residents was just a modified form of colonies.

The Democratic Party of Korea held the Emergency Central Committee on the 27th of December,
Have decided to develop a national movement with the resolution of absolute anti- trusteeship.

신탁 통치 반대

제국주의의 영토 확장의 수단이었던 식민지가
이주 식민지에서 착취 식민지로 정책이 바뀌었네

일본 제국주의는 보호 조약을 빌미로 약소국을 예속시켜
반식민지화하여 사회 및 경제적 수탈을 자행했네

식민지이면서도 식민지가 아닌 것처럼
위장한 위임 통치委任統治나 신탁 통치信託統治는
연합국이 패전국을 통치하는 통치 수단이었네

제1차 세계 대전 승전국이 행사한 위임 통치나
제2차 세계 대전 승전국이 주민의 자치, 독립을 촉진하기 위해
추진한 국제 연합의 신탁 통치지信託統治地 제도는
변형된 식민지의 한 형태에 불과했네

긴급중앙집행위원회를 개최한 한국민주당은(1945. 12. 27.)
신탁 통치 절대 배격 결의문과 함께
국민 운동을 전개하기로 했네

The Provisional Government held the emergency cabinet meeting Inviting political parties, religious organizations, and media organizations Decided to form the National People's Solidarity Committee against the Trusteeship.

Cho So-ang, the foreign minister of the Provisional Government declared a fighting against the trusteeship on the 28th of December.

The National People's Solidarity Commission against the trusteeship sent a resolution letter of anti-trusteeship to the attention of the summits of four nations.
After resolving the implementation of the 12 clauses through the central committee meeting insisted to have immediate sovereignty of the Provisional Government on the 29th of December.

There were reports and press conference several times by Vincent of the US Secretary of State,
Rhee Syng-man was said that he predicted the trusteeship urged to express our resolution not to be cheated by the carrot to shorten the term of 5 years trusteeship on the 29th of December.

Kim Gu called the emergency cabinet meeting of the Provisional Government on the 29th of December and declared that there is nothing left to do but all nation's fighting against trusteeship.

긴급국무회의를 개최한 임시 정부는
각 정당, 종교 단체, 언론 기관을 초청하여
신탁통치반대 국민총동원위원회의 구성을 결의했네 「註釋*24」

임시 정부의 조소앙趙素昻 외무장관은 담화를 통해(1945. 12. 28.)
신탁 통치 반대 투쟁을 선언했네

신탁통치반대 국민총동원위원회는 연합국 4국 원수에게
신탁 통치 반대 결의문을 발송하고
12개 항의 반탁 국민 동원 실행 방법을 결의한 후
중앙 위원 회의를 통해
임시 정부의 즉각적 주권 행사를 건의했네(1945. 12. 29.)

미 국무성 빈센트 씨가
누차 서한과 기자 회견을 통해 보도한 바 있어
신탁 통치를 예측했다는 이승만은
5개 년 단축시키라는 감언에 속지 말고
우리의 결심을 표명할 것을 촉구했네(1945. 12. 29.)

김구는 임시 정부의 긴급 국무 회의를 소집하여(1945. 12. 29.)
전 민족이 투쟁할 일만이 남아 있다고 선언했네

Ahn Jae-hong, the Nationalist Party leader declared total uprising stating that trusteeship is Process of making Korea a communist regime on the 29th of December.

Lee Yeo-sung of the People's Party insisted that trusteeship should be opposed by diplomatic line.

The Independence Group insisted to demonstrate at large supported by the Provisional Government with the motto "There is no independence with no fighting and there will never be liberty with no blood. Let's advance all of us to the road of fighting in blood". They urged to hold Korean flags and advance chanting 'viva independence' on the 29th of December.

All the de lux restaurants and bars closed doors and opposed to the trusteeship.

All of the lawyers in the Civil and Criminal section of the Justice department, 3 courts and 3 inspection departments were absolutely obedient to the order of the Provisional Government and they entered into a general strike at 14:00 hours 29th of December.

All the Korean staffs in the Military Government office resolved the resignation and committed a general strike on the 29th of December.
On the 30th of December, more than 3,000 Korean employees participated in this demonstration.

안재홍安在鴻 국민당 당수는
신탁 통치는 조선의 적화赤化 기도 공작이라며
총궐기를 선언했네(1945. 12. 29.)

인민당(이여성)은 신탁 통치는
외교로 투쟁해야 한다고 주장했네

임시 정부를 중심으로 대시위 운동을 전개하자는 광복단은
"전쟁 없는 독립은 없고
피 뿌리지 않는 자유는 결단코 없는 것이다.
나가자! 너 나 없이 피의 싸움길로."
라는 구호 아래 태극기를 들고
독립 만세를 부르며 나가자고 촉구했네(1945. 12. 29.)

요정과 바도 일제히 문을 닫고 신탁 통치를 반대했네

법무국 민, 형사과와 3법원과 3검사국 등 재야 법조인은
임시 정부 명령에 절대 복종하여
12월 29일 오후 2시, 총파업을 단행했네

군정청 조선인 직원은 총사직을 결의하고
12월 30일, 총파업을 결행
군정청 조선인 직원 삼천여 명이 시위에 참가했네

On the 30th of December, under Provisional Government, the "National People's Solidarity Committee" was set up for independence opposing trusteeship with the motto "Let's have bloody fight even to the last person".

More than 40 organizations demanded approval of the Provisional Government and resolved the general strike. The domestic branch of the Kwangbok (means Liberation) military corps declared to take an independence of the fatherland in spite of their death.

Kim Gu's scheduled broadcasting at 20 hours of the 29th December with the title of "We are against the trusteeship" in the Seoul Central Broadcasting System was suddenly stopped.

All the Korean employees in the Seoul City Hall responded to the aspiration of opposing the trusteeship and all of them immediately resolved their resignation.

The Provisional Government of the Republic of Korea has announced under name of Shin Ik-hee, The minister of Domestic Affairs in the proclamation of Kukja No. 1 and 2 on the 31st of December that "The Korean staffs and police in the US Military Government should follow the order of the Provisional Government".

Many chiefs of the police stations in Seoul visited Kim Gu and Provisional Government and swore their loyalty.

12월 30일, 임시 정부 지휘로
"최후의 일인까지 혈투하자."
는 신탁 통치 반대, 독립 쟁취를 위한
'국민총동원위원회' 가 설치됐네

40여 단체가 대동 단결 임시 정부 승인을 요구하며
총파업을 결의했네
광복군 국내 지대가 결사보국으로 독립 쟁취를 선언했네

"우리는 신탁 통치를 반대한다."
는 제목으로 예정되었던(1945. 12. 29. 하오 8시)
김구의 서울중앙방송국 방송이 돌연 중지됐네

서울시청 조선인 직원 전원은 신탁 통치 반대 기세에
부응하여 전 직원이 즉시 총사직을 결의했네

대한민국 임시 정부는 신익희申翼熙 내무부장 명의로 발표한
국자國字 1호와 2호 포고문에서(1945. 12. 31.) 「註釋*25」
"미 군정의 조선인 관리와 경찰들은
임시 정부의 명령에 따라야 한다."고 선포했네

서울시내 다수의 경찰서장들이
김구와 임시 정부를 찾아가 충성을 맹세했네

It was a manifestation of the will to exercise substantive ruling of the Provisional Government denying the sovereignty of the US Military Government.

Lieutenant General Hodge, the commander of the US Military Government, defined it as a coup, strongly warned Kim Gu and the Provisional Government on the 1st of January, 1946.

The premier Kim Gu of the Provisional Government urged demonstrators to return to their works on the 1st of January, 1946 saying "The anti-trusteeship movement is only anti-trusteeship and not anti-military government".

On the 4th of January, the Provisional Government intended to call an emergency political meeting to succeed it as a transitional top legislative body and organized the Preparatory Committee for Emergency Political Societies.

According to the Chongqing's declaration of the Provisional Government's Present Policy No. 6 in September, 1945,

They tried to rule out the trusteeship "To establish the formal government convening National Representative Convention, and set the constitutional law after establishing a transitional regime by holding an emergency political meeting covering the representatives from domestic and overseas with the Provisional Government as the center.

미 군정의 통치권을 부정하고 임시 정부가
실질적 통치를 행사하겠다는 의지의 표명이었네

미 군정 사령관 하지 중장은 이를 쿠데타로 규정하고
김구와 임시 정부에 강력히 경고했네(1946. 01. 01.)

이에 임시 정부의 김구 주석은 엄항섭嚴恒燮 선전부장을 통해
"신탁 통치 반대 운동은 탁치 반대이지 군정 반대는 아니다."
며 시위자들에게 직장으로 복귀할 것을 촉구했네(1946. 01. 01.)

1월 4일, 임시 정부는 임정을 계승할
과도적 최고 입법 기관으로 비상 정치 회의를 소집하기로 하고
비상정치회의주비회非常政治會議籌備會를
조직했네「註釋*26」

충칭重慶에서 발표한(1945. 09.)
임시 정부 당면 정책 제6항에 의거

"임시 정부를 중심으로 국내외 각계 각층 대표들이 참여한
비상정치회의를 개최하여 과도 정권을 수립한 후에
국민대표대회를 소집하여 헌법을 제정하고
정식 정부를 수립"
하여 신탁 통치를 배제하고자 했네

The Provisional Government selected 5 ministers to convene an emergency political meeting;

Kim Yak-san (nickname Kim Won-bong), Kim Sung-sook, Cho So-ang, Cho Wan-gu and Chang Geon-sang. They appointed them as public relations officers, and negotiated with every political party member both right or left wing and all walks of life.

Hong Nam-pyo, the bargaining representative from the side of the People's Republic of Korea,showed intransigent attitude under the pretext that the Provisional Government side was domineering attitude and was insincere on the unification matter.

However, prior to the opening of the US and Soviet Joint Committee,it was difficult for them to disregard the justification of unified action by political parties either left or right.

The four party representatives of the Democratic Party of Korea, the Nationalist Party, the People's Party and the Communist Party discussed on the basic policy of achieving national unification through repeated individual contacts and finally they agreed each other on the 7th of January.

Four political parties announced joint statement;
"With regard to the decision on the matter of Korea in the three nations' foreign ministers meeting at Moscow, we wholly agree with the spirit and intention to guarantee the independence of Korea and to help its democratic

비상정치회의 소집을 위하여 김약산金若山 (일명 金元鳳)
김성숙金星淑, 조소앙, 조완구趙琬九, 장건상張建相 등
국무 위원 5명을 대외 교섭 위원으로 선정한 임시 정부는
좌, 우익 각 정당 및 각 계 인사들을 교섭했네

인민공화국측의 교섭 대표 홍남표洪南杓는
임시 정부 측이 군림적 태도와 통일에 대해
무성의하다는 이유로 비타협적인 태도를 보였네

그러나 미소공동위원회의 개회를 앞두고
각 정당 간 행동 통일이라는 대의 명분을
좌, 우익 어느 쪽도 외면하기 어려웠네

한국민주당, 국민당, 인민당, 공산당의 4당 대표들이
여러 차례 개별적 접촉을 통해 민족 통일 성취에 대한
기본 방침을 토의한 결과
의견의 일치를 보게 되었네(1946. 01. 07.)

"모스크바 삼상 회의의 조선 문제 결정에 대하여
조선의 자주 독립을 보장하고 민주주의적 발전을 원조한다는
정신과 의도를 전면적으로 지지한다.
국제연합헌장에 의하여 의구疑懼되는 신탁 제도는
장래 수립될 우리 정부로 하여금

development. The trusteeship system that is suspected by the Charter of the United Nations to be solved under the basis of self-independent spirit by the Korean government to be established in the future."

Five political parties including New Korea National Party and Provisional Government people participated in the repeated discussion in relation with the basic policy of national unification on the 9th of January finally resulted to failure. The Provisional Government people insisted to link this 5 political parties meeting to the preparatory meeting of emergency political meeting and the communist party insisted to support the decision made in the three foreign ministers meeting.

Provisional Government decided to hold the first preparatory meeting of the emergency political meeting as scheduled originally after having ministers' meeting with participation of one representative each from 18 organizations, and 3 representatives from the Provisional Government as observers during the 20th～24th of January excluding the Communist Party of Korea, the People's Party and the Independent Alliance.

The US Military Government authority ordered General Lerch to stop the Provisional Government trying to convene emergency political meeting or establishing an independent transitional government on the 18th of January.

자주 독립의 정신에 기基하여 해결하게 한다."
는 4당 공동 성명을 발표하였네

신한민족당新韓民族黨까지 참가한
5대 정당과 임시 정부 요인들이
민족 통일에 대한 기본 방침을 중심으로
토의를 거듭하였으나(1946. 01. 09.)
5당 대표 회의를 비상정치회의의 예비 회담으로 결부하려는
임시 정부 측 주장과 삼상 회의 결정의 전면적 지지를 고집한
공산당의 주장이 대립하여 결렬되고 말았네

임정 측은 본래의 계획대로 임시 정부 국무 회의를 거쳐
조선 공산당, 인민당과 독립 동맹을 제외한
18개 단체의 대표 각 1명씩과 임시 정부 측 위원 3명이
옵서버로 참석하여 비상정치회의의
제1차 준비 회의를 개최하기로 했네(1946. 01. 20.~24.)

미 군정 당국은 러치 장군에게
임시 정부의 비상 정치 회의 소집이나
독자적인 과도 정부 수립 시도를
저지하라는 훈령을 내렸네(1946. 01. 18.)

Park Hun-young, honorary chief of the National Council of Korean Trade Unions held an emergency committee and announced a statement against the trusteeship on the 30th of December.

Park Hun Young visited the Soviet consulate after hearing news of the three ministers meeting in Moscow. He heard that there was no instruction from his home country and crossed 38 parallel line at night on the 28th of December.

Park Hun-young had a second meeting with Kim Il-sung on the 29th of December. After two days he attended at the North Korean Communist Party executive committee on the 31st of December where the deputy commander Romanenko in charge of civil and political affairs in the Soviet Union's Military Government and Polyanski, the general consul in Seoul.

In spite of Park Hun-young's report that Seoul's opposition of trusteeship was unexpectedly strong, the Soviet's instruction was in favor of the trusteeship.

The Soviet judged that the Communist Party would be numerically superior in the composition of Provisional Government, because the left wing power in South Korea and that of North Korea would be absolutely powerful even though the US and Soviet joint committee would be held.

박헌영朴憲永이 명예 위원장으로 있는
조선노동조합전국평의회는 「註釋*27」
긴급 위원회를 개최하고
신탁 통치 반대 성명을 발표했네(1945. 12. 30.)

박헌영은 모스크바 삼상 회의 뉴스를 듣고
소련 영사관을 찾았으나,
본국의 훈령이 없다는 답을 듣자
그날 밤 38선을 넘었네(1945. 12. 28.)

12월 29일, 김일성과 두 번째 면담을 한 박헌영은
이틀 후 소련 군정 민정 담당 부사령관 로마넨코와
서울 총영사 폴리얀스키가 참석한
북조선 공산당 집행위원회에 참석했네(1945. 12. 31.)

서울의 반탁 주장이 예상 외로 거세다는 보고에도 불구하고
소련의 지침은 신탁 통치 찬성이었네

남한의 좌익 세력과 북한을 합치면
남한의 나머지 세력에 비해 절대적 우위이기 때문에
미소공동위원회가 열리더라도 임시 정부의 구성에서

Park Hun-young who returned to Seoul after being instructed by the Soviet Military Government on January 2, 1946, expressed his official attitude through the Central Committee of the Communist Party of Korea having instruction that the agreement of the three foreign ministers meeting in Moscow was not a 'trusteeship' but a 'guardianship'.

"The three foreign ministers' meeting in Moscow was a step forward for the development of global democracy and the establishment of a democratic Provisional Government in Korea is the most legitimate for Korea. The five-year term of the trusteeship is owing to our people and our turning this responsibility over to the three countries, and to disobey it?will be very dangerous consequences for Korea."

The Seoul Citizens' Meeting against the Trusteeship was jointly held by the Seoul Citizens Committee and the Anti-fascist Joint Fighting Committee at 1:00 pm at the Seoul Sports Complex.

Just before the opening ceremony, the name of the event was changed to 'The Citizens' Meeting of Urging the National Unification for Self-Independence', and the speech was like that of three foreign ministers meeting instead of against the trusteeship.

The communists mobilized by the organizers started to cry out the slogans such as "Absolute Support for the Foreign Ministers' Meeting", "Defend People's Republic to the death" "verthrow Kim Gu and Rhee Syng-man" and "Immediately Stop Strike of Closing Stores" etc.

공산당이 수적으로 우세할 것으로 소련은 판단했네
모스크바 삼상 회의 합의가 '신탁 통치' 가 아닌 '후견제' 라는
소련 군정의 지시를 받고 서울로 돌아온 박헌영은(1946. 01. 02.)
조선공산당 중앙 위원회를 통해 공식적인 태도를 표명했네

"모스크바 3상 회의는 세계 민주주의 발전에 있어서
한 걸음 진보한 것이며
한국에 민주적 임시 정부를 수립하는 것은
조선을 위하는 가장 정당한 것이다.
신탁 통치의 5년 기한은 우리 민족의 탓인데
이 책임을 3국에 돌리고 반대 배격하는 것은
조선을 위하여 극히 위험천만한 결과를 나타낼 것이다."

서울시인민위원회, 투쟁위원회 등이
공동 주최한 신탁 통치반대 서울시민대회가
오후 1시, 서울 운동장에서 열렸네

개회 직전, 대회 이름은
'민족통일 자주 촉성 시민대회' 로 바뀌고
신탁 통치 반대 연설 대신 3상 회의 취지의 연설이 이어졌네

주최측이 동원한 공산당원들이

Angry citizens were carrying the placard of 'We are absolutely against Trusteeship'.

The Commander Chistyakov of the Soviet Military Government called Cho Man-sik, head of the Democratic Party of Korea on December 30, 1945 and strongly persuaded him to declare supporting statement in the name of the Democratic Party of Korea but in vain.

Cho Man-sik convened the Central Committee of the Democratic Party of Korea on January 2, 1946 with nine members of the communist line absent adopted the resolution of
"We can never agree with the trusteeship" in the name of the Democratic Party of Korea.

First lieutenant general Romannenko offered to Cho Man-sik, "If you only announce a statement in favor of the guardianship, I will take Kim Il-sung as the head of the military, and invite you as the first president" but he could not persuade Cho Man-sik.

After meeting Cho Man-sik, the angry Kim Il-sung suggested to Romannenko

"Let's kill this stubborn old guy on this occasion."
But the Soviet Military Government rejected this suggestion that they could not carry a bomb in the process of revolution.

'외상 회의 절대 지지', '인민 공화국 사수'
'김구, 이승만 타도', '철시 파업 즉시 중단'
등의 구호를 외치기 시작했네

화가 난 시민들은
'신탁 통치 절대 반대' 플래카드를 들고 나섰네

소련 군정 치스차코프 사령관은
조선민주당 당수 조만식을 불러서(1945. 12. 30.)
조선민주당이 지지 성명을 내줄 것을
강력히 설득했으나 실패했네

공산주의 계열의 위원 9명이 불참한 가운데
조선민주당 중앙 위원회를 소집한 조만식(1946. 01. 02.)은
"신탁 통치를 절대 찬성할 수 없다."
는 결의문을 조선민주당 이름으로 채택했네

로마넨코 소장은 "후견제를 찬성하는 성명서만 발표해 준다면
김일성을 군부책임자로, 선생을 초대 대통령으로 모시겠다."
제의했지만 조만식을 설득할 수 없었네

조만식을 만난 후 분노한 김일성이 로마넨코에게
"이 기회에 고집쟁이 영감을 죽여 버리자." 건의했지만

Under the leadership of the Soviet Union, the Pyeongnam People's Committee was urgently called at 11:00 am on the 5th of January.

First lieutenant Lebedev explained the plan of trusteeship and as soon as pro-trusteeship speech was over by communist delegates, they demanded to chairman Cho Man-sik to resolve pro-trusteeship.
Chairman Cho Man-sik definitely refused to accept it saying

"As I belong to the Democratic Party of Korea, I refuse it.
My national conscience doesn't allow me to deal with this problem casually,
and I can't vote on it until we have enough discussions."
He refused definitely.

From the seats of the Soviet leaders, there was a screaming "Then you resign the chairmanship."

"Whether or not we support the trusteeship, opinions should be expressed freely by Koreans.

What does it mean to just favor the trusteeship? Even though we are under Military Government,restricting the press or expressing one's opinion is against the democratic principle.
No matter what the reason may be, trusteeship is interfering to the other country's politics.
It is natural that we claim our sovereignty and interests."

혁명 과정에서 폭탄을 안고 갈 수 없다며 소련 군정이 반대했네

소련 군정 주도하에
평남인민위원회가 긴급 소집되었네(1946. 01. 05.)

레베데프 소장이 신탁 통치안을 설명하고
이어진 공산당 측 위원들의 탁치 찬성 발언이 끝나자
그들은 조만식 의장에게 신탁 통치 찬성 결의를 요구했네

조만식 의장은

"나는 조선민주당 소속이기 때문에 반대한다.
나의 민족적 양심이 이 문제를 경솔히 다루는 것을
허락하지 않을뿐더러 충분히 토의하기 전에는
절대 표결에 부칠 수 없다."
며 단호히 거부했네

소련 군정 지도부석에서
"그러면 의장직을 사임하라."
는 고함이 들렸네

"신탁을 찬성하든 반대하든 모든 의사는
우리 조선인의 자유여야 한다.

Cho Man-sik resigned as Chairman of the Pyeongnam People's Committee.

The Soviet military government officially accepted the resignation of Cho Man-sik,
And unanimously passed the resolutions of the pro-trusteeship by representing Hong Ki-joo as the temporary chairman.

From this day on, Cho Man-sik was detained at the Koryo Hotel.

Cho Man-sik met with Anhur C Bunce on October 5, 1946 when Bunce visited Pyongyang as a member of the US Military Government at the US Soviet Joint Committee. Cho Man-sik was imprisoned in Pyongyang prison. He was shot to death together with 500 political prisoners by retreating North Korean soldiers during the Korean War on October 18, 1950.

Rhee Syng-man, agreed with Kim Gu, explained the hostile position of the US Military Government against the emergency political meeting at the first preparatory meeting of the emergency political meeting during $20^{th} \sim 24^{th}$ of January. They reorganized the 'Emergency National Assembly' by mixing the Central Council for Urging Independence and the Emergency Political Conference together on the 23rd of January.

Three persons Kim Yak-san and Sung Joo-sik of the Korean Nationalist Revolutionary Party,

신탁에 찬성만 하라는 것은 무슨 뜻인가?
아무리 군정이라도 언론이나 의사 표시를 제한하는 것은
민주주의 원칙에 벗어난다.
무슨 구실을 붙이더라도 신탁 통치라는 것은
남의 나라 정치에 간섭하는 것이다.
우리가 우리의 주권과 이익을 주장하는 것은
너무나 당연하다."
고 말한 조만식은 평남인민위원회 의장직을 사임했네

소련 군정은 조만식의 평남인민정치위 의장직 사표를
정식으로 수리하고,
임시 의장에 홍기주洪箕疇를 내세워서
신탁 통치 찬성 결의를 만장일치로 통과시켰네

이 날부터 조만식은 고려 호텔에 연금되었네

미소공동위원회 미 군정측 일행으로 평양을 방문한
번스(Anhur C Bunce)와 만난(1946. 10. 05.) 조만식은
평양 형무소에 수감되었다가 한국전쟁 때
퇴각하는 북한군에 의해 정치범 500명과 함께
총살당했네(1950. 10. 18.)

비상정치회의의 제1차 준비 회의(1946. 01. 20.～24.)에서

Kim Sung-sook of the Korean National Liberation Alliance and Jang Geon-sang of the Provisional Government broke up with the Provisional Government and dropped out of the Emergency National Assembly.

When the organizations under Communist Party refused to participate in the Emergency National Assembly, the Emergency National Assembly excluded leftist forces, elected 28 members of the highest governance committee and assumed to organize the system of the highest governance members to Rhee Syng-man, Kim Gu and Kim Kyu-sik on the 1st of February.

At the request of the US Military Government, the Emergency National Assembly changed the title of the highest governance committee into Democratic Lawmaker.
And they reorganized it into the National Democratic Representative of South Korea to represent as an advisors' organization for the US Military Government instead of decision-making organization on the 14th of February.

The National Democratic Representative of South Korea was held three times a week at Changduk Palace. They discussed the agenda to submit to US Soviet Joint Committee in relation with all the matters.
When the first US Soviet Joint Committee was held, Rhee Syng-man resigned as chairman insisting the South Korea's sole government.

Kim Kyu-sik, acted as substitute chairman, tried to have a movement of

비상정치회의에 대한
미 군정의 적대적 입장을 설명한 이승만은 김구와 합의하에
독립촉성중앙협의회獨立促成中央協議會와
비상정치회의를 통합하여 '비상국민회의非常國民會議' 로
개편했네(1946. 01. 23.)「註釋*28」

임정의 혁신 계열인 조선민족혁명당의 김약산(일명 김원봉),
성주식成周寔 및 조선민족해방동맹의 김성숙 등 3명과
임시 정부의 장건상은 임시 정부와 결별하고
비상국민회의를 탈퇴하였네

공산당 산하 단체가 비상국민회의 참가를 거부하자
좌파 세력이 배제된 비상국민회의는 과도 정권 수립을 위한
28명의 최고 정무 위원을 선출하고, 정무 위원회 조직 구성을
이승만, 김구, 김규식 3인에게 일임하였네(1946. 02. 01.)

비상국민회의는 미 군정의 요청으로 최고 정무 위원 명칭을
의결 기관이 아닌 군정청 자문 기관인 남조선
대한국민대표 민주의원으로 개편했네(1946. 02. 14.)「註釋*29」

남조선 대한국민대표 민주의원은 매주 3회 창덕궁에서
회의를 열고 미소공동위원회에 관한 제반 문제를 검토하여
민족 진영이 제출할 안건을 토의했네

joint left, right wings.
As a result, the function of the National Democratic Representative of South Korea was suspended.

Most of the politicians and US Military Government officials who welcomed Rhee Syng-man's repatriation expected to present the generous political policy to embrace even the hostile leaders.

They wanted to utilize the reputation of the old politician in their 70's for their own purposesand wanted them to remain a symbolic politician only.

The US Military Government had confidence that if Rhee Syng-man were invited to a high ranking position, it would be possible to lead him to support the US Military Government.

The US Department of State forced Rhee Syng-man to have complete independence after having transitional government first saying that it would be possible in Korea by means of compromise that the US and Soviet failed to make it in East Europe.

Winston Churchill had a lecture on the 5th of March at a small university in Fulton, Missouri;
He had a historical speech "The entire region of Eastern Europe has become prison when the iron curtain covered the whole Europe. Due to the Soviet ambition of endless hegemony and expansion of communism, the world is under threat."

제1차 미소공동위원회가 개최되자 신탁 통치를 반대하던
이승만은 의장직을 사퇴하고 남한만의 단독 정부를 주장했네

대리 의장직을 맡은 김규식이 좌우 합작 운동을 추진하자
남조선 대한국민대표 민주의원의 기능은 정지되었네

이승만의 환국을 환영했던 수많은 정치인들과 미 군정은
이승만이 적대적인 지도자까지 포용하는 정강 정책을
내놓을 것으로 기대했네

70대 고령인 이승만의 명성을 자신들의 목적에 이용하기 위해
그가 상징적인 정치인으로 남아 있기를 원했네

미 군정은 고위직으로 이승만을 추대하면
미 군정에 대한 지지를 이끌어 낼 수 있으리라 확신했네

미 국무부는 미국과 소련이 동유럽에서
이루어 내지 못한 타협을 한국에서는
이루어 낼 수 있다며, 연립 과도 정부를 거친 후
완전한 독립을 이승만에게 강요했네

윈스턴 처칠은 미주리 주 풀턴의 한 대학 강연(1946. 03. 05.)에서

Rhee Syng-man opposed to the US policy on the Korean peninsula insisting that its policy is to replace the ownership of Korea to communists from Japanese rule.

It was because of his conviction that the compromising with communism will inevitably result in surrender to communism.

The friendship between the general Hodge and Rhee Syng-man, which was called "My best friend ever" was over, and the conflicts between the two friends were started to appear publicly.

Molotov, the Soviet foreign affairs minister, sent an order to the Soviet Military Government in relation with the establishment of the Democratic Provisional Government of Korea on the 16th of March.

The order was "To proceed in two steps to draw up an agreement on the members of the Democratic Provisional Government of Korea in accordance with the decision of the three foreign ministers meeting in Moscow and to take measures on Korean people's politic, economic, social development, aid and guardian matter, and to establish the national sovereignty of Korea."

"철의 장막(iron curtain) 「**註釋*30**」이 전 유럽에 드리워지자
동유럽의 전 지역은 감옥 상태로 변했다.
소련의 '끝없는 패권주의와 공산주의 확장' 이라는
야욕 때문에 전 세계가 위협을 받고 있다."
는 역사적인 연설을 했네

이승만은 미국의 한반도 정책이 한국의 주인을
일본에서 공산주의자로 교체하는 정책이라면서 반대했네

공산주의와의 타협은 필연적으로 공산주의에
항복하는 결과를 가져올 것이라는 확신 때문이었네

"우리의 가장 좋은 친구"라고 평했던
하지 장군과 이승만의 우정은 끝이 나고
두 사람의 갈등이 공개적으로 표출되기 시작했네

소련 외무성 장관 몰로토프는 조선 민주주의 임시 정부 수립에
관련해 소련 군정 사령부에 지령을 보냈네(1946. 03. 16.)

"모스크바 삼상 회의 결정에 따라
조선 민주주의 임시 정부 구성원에 대한 합의서를 작성하고,
조선 인민의 정치, 경제, 사회적 발전과 원조에 대한
후견 조치를 강구하여

The Soviet Union already completed the organization of the "South and North Provisional Government Cabinet Plan" on the 7th of March before the opening of the Committee with anticipation that the Provisional Government cabinet plan would be smoothly agreed at the first round meeting of the US-Soviet Joint Committee.

The Soviet Union organized the left-wing led cabinet under the plan to make the whole Korean peninsula be under the Soviet influence with the Provisional Government in parliamentary cabinet system and organized first cabinet;

Yeo Wun-hyung as prime minister, Park Hun-young and Kim Kyu-sik as deputy prime ministers, Huh Hun as foreign minister and Kim Il-sung as domestic affairs minister.

민주주의적 발전과 조선의 국가적 자주권을
확립하는 두 단계로 구분해 진행하라."
는 지시였네

소련은 제1차 미소공동위원회에서
내각제 임시 정부 수립안이 원만하게 합의될 것을 예상하고
위원회가 열리기 전에
'남북 임시 정부 내각안' 을
수립, 조각까지 마친 상태였네(1946. 03. 07.)

소련은 좌익이 주도한 내각 책임제 임시 정부로
한반도 전체를 소비에트화한다는 계획 아래
수상에 여운형, 부수상에 박헌영과 김규식, 외무상에 허헌
내무상에 김일성 등으로 초대 내각을 짜 놓았네

US-Soviet Joint Committee

The Korean Democratic Party Jang Duk-soo who solved the internal conflict in the party when Song Jin-woo was murdered, he recommended Inchon Kim Seong-soo as the head of general affairs and he himself became the political director of the party.

Chang Duk-su insisted that they should actively participate in the US-Soviet Joint Committee in order to express opinion of the Korean people saying to not only Rhee Syng-man and Kim Gu but also to Kim Sung-soo of Korea Democratic Party who opposes Chang's opinion on account of pursuing the trusteeship by US-Soviet Joint Committee.

The theory of Chang Duk-soo was, at present situation, we can't get rid of influence of the United States and the Soviet Union for the independence of Korea, and we don't have enough strength to get rid of their power.

When the first US-Soviet Joint Committee was decided to open, Chang Duk-soo visited Rhee Syng-man and Kim Gu, and strongly persuaded them to participate in the US-Soviet Joint Committee Meeting but it was rejected.

They argued fiercely by screaming between Kim Gu and Chang Duk-soo.

미소공동위원회

송진우가 암살된 후 혼란에 빠진 한국민주당의 내분을 수습한
장덕수張德秀는 인촌仁村 김성수金成洙를 수석총무로 추대하고
한민당韓民黨의 정치부장으로 선출되었네 「註釋*31」

미소공동위원회美蘇共同委員會를
반대하는 이승만, 김구, 김성수 등에게
장덕수는 한국인의 견해를 당당히 표명하기 위해서는
미소공동위원회에 적극 참석해야 한다는 주장을 했네

현재는 한국의 독립이
미국과 소련의 입김을 배제시킬 수 없는 상황이며
우리의 힘 또한 이들을 밀어내기는 역부족이라는 것이
장덕수의 지론이었네

제1차 미소공동위원회가 결정되자 장덕수는
이승만과 김구를 찾아가서 미소공동위원회에 참가할 것을
강력히 설득했으나 거절당했네

김구와 장덕수 사이에는 격렬한 고성까지 오고갔네

The representatives of the US-Soviet Joint Meeting (US-Soviet Joint Committee Preliminary Meeting) major general, Arnold, A. V. of the United States, and lieutenant general, Shtikov, T. E. of Soviet had a meeting at the Sukjojun building, Duksoo Palace on the 16th of January.

They discussed on the matters of economic and administrative caused by the division of Koreaand announced a joint statement on the 5th of February "To establish the US-Soviet Joint Committee within a month" after a difficult discussion due to the differences in the positions of both sides.

The First US-Soviet Joint Committee was held in Seoul on March 20, 1946.

The Soviet Union, as a criterion for the selection of candidates for consultation in Korea,

suggested three points to support the decision of the three foreign ministers meeting in Moscow, to be truly democratic, and should not be an anti-Soviet group or individual.

As most of the Koreans oppose the decision of the three foreign ministers meeting, US opposed to this stating that it is not fair to decide to exclude the opposing persons from the candidates on account of the reason that they oppose the trusteeship.

The US-Soviet Joint Committee announced 'No.5 Communiqué on the 17th April.'

미국의 아놀드 소장과 소련의 스티코프 중장이
각각 대표를 맡은 미소공동위원회 예비 회담이
덕수궁 석조전에서 개최되었네(1946. 01. 16.)

분단으로 인한 경제, 행정상의 문제를 집중 논의했으나
양측의 입장 차이로 난항 끝에
"1개월 이내 미소공동위원회를 설치한다."
는 공동 성명을 발표하고 폐회했네(1946. 02. 05.)

제1차 미소공동위원회는
서울에서 개최되었네(1946. 03.20.)

소련측은 임시 정부 수립을 위한 협의 대상자 선정 기준으로
모스크바 3상 회의 결정을 지지할 것
진실로 민주주의적이어야 할 것
반소련 집단이나 인물이 아닐 것 등 세 가지를 제시했네

미국측은 한국인의 대부분은 3상 회의 결정을
반대하고 있기 때문에 신탁 통치에 반대한다는 이유로
협의 대상에서 제외하는 것은 부당하다고 맞섰네

미소공동위원회는
'제5호 코뮤니케' 를 발표했네(1946. 04.17.) 「註釋*32」

The US-Soviet Joint Committee declared the statement that the political parties and organizations "Need to sign to promise to support the three foreign ministers agreement made in Moscow"

However, the first US-Soviet Joint Committee declared an indefinite recess on the 6th May because they couldn't narrow the different position which was derived from whether or not the signing the declaration was meaning of accepting the trusteeship or not.

When the first US-Soviet Joint Committee ended in failure
Rhee Syng-man, who gave up the position of chairman of the National Democratic Party of South Korea travelled for speech all around South Korea, spoke political speech at Jeong-eup on the 3rd of June;

"There is no sign of resumption of the US-Soviet Joint Committee which is in indefinite recess and we can't have an expectation of the unified government against our wish.
Therefore we had better to appeal to world public opinion to make the withdrawal of the Soviet Union from the north of 38 parallel by organizing the Provisional Government or organization even in South Korea only."

Rhee Syng-man's topic of speech while travelling all around South Korea was always the same.

협의 대상이 될 정당과 단체는

"모스크바 삼국 외상 회의 협정에 대한 지지를
 약속하는 선언서에 서명해야 한다."
는 미소공동위원회 성명이었네

그러나 선언서에 서명을 하는 것이
신탁 통치를 받아들이겠다는 것을 뜻하는 것인지
아닌지의 여부를 두고 발생한 입장 차이를 좁히지 못한 채
제1차 미소공동위원회는 무기 휴회를 선언했네(1946. 05. 06.)

제1차 미소공동위원회가 실패로 끝나자
남조선대한국민대표민주의원 의장직을 내던진 이승만은
남한 각지를 돌며 순회 연설하던 중 정읍에서

"무기 휴회된 미소공동위원회가 재개될 기색도 보이지 않으며
 통일 정부를 고대하나 여의치 않으니 남한만이라도
 임시 정부, 혹은 위원회 같은 것을 조직하여 38 이북에서
 소련을 철퇴하도록 세계 공론에 호소하여야 될 것이다."
는 정치적 발언을 했네(1946. 06. 03.)「註釋*33」

남한 전역을 돌면서 유세하는 이승만의 연설 주제는
언제나 똑같았네

"Communism is like a horrific epidemic cholera."
"With communism, there is no compromise or negotiation. The only choice is to surrender to the communist dictatorship or to resist to it.
The only way to save Korean democracy is to absolutely reject trusteeship and communism."

Many Americans residing in Korea have applauded Rhee Syng-man's campaign but the US Military Government and the US State Department resented which were responsible to try to find a way to implement the Moscow Trusteeship Agreement"

As soon as the first round of the Joint Committee was suspended, the Soviet Communist Party postponed the idea of establishing a provisional government, Stalin ordered on concrete measures in the fields of economy, industry, technology, broadcasting, education, military, medical to the ministries concerned of the cabinet and to the Soviet army on July 26, 1946 to establish a sole government in North Korea.

'The counterfeiting case of the Chosun Jeongpansa Company' was announced in the name of the Chang Taek-sang, chief of the National Police Agency on the 15th of May.

"공산주의는 무서운 전염병인 콜레라와 같다.
공산주의와는 타협이나 협상이 불가능하다.
유일한 선택은 공산 독재주의에 굴복할 것인가
저항할 것인가 하는 것뿐이다.
한국 민주주의를 구원할 수 있는 유일한 길은
신탁 통치와 공산주의를 철저히 거부하는 길뿐이다."

한국에 거주하는 많은 미국인들은
이승만의 캠페인에 박수를 보냈지만
모스크바 신탁 통치 협정을 이행할 방법을 찾아야 하는
책임을 지고 있던 미 군정과 국무부는 분개했네

제1차 미소공동위원회가 중단되자
즉시 중앙위원회를 개최한 소련공산당은
남북 조선 임시정부 수립 구상을 뒤로 미루고
북조선에 단독 정부를 설립하라는 스탈린의 지령에 따른
경제, 산업, 기술, 방송, 교육, 군사, 의료 등의 분야에 대한
결정된 구체적인 방안을 내각의 해당 부처와
소련군 산하에 지령했네(1946. 07. 26.)

'조선정판사朝鮮精版社 위폐僞幣 사건' 전모가
장택상張澤相 경찰청장의 이름으로
발표되었네(1946. 05. 15.)「註釋*34」

“The banknote counterfeit group members were rounded up who disturbed whole South Korea with counterfeit bills of more than 3 million won. In the banknote counterfeit members group was composed of two officers of the Korea Communist Party and another fourteen members of it were workers of Chosun Jeongpansa Company.
The Chosun Jeongpansa Company was located in the Geuntaek Building which was used for the headquarters of the Korea Communist Party. This company was printing Haebang Ilbo Daily which was the nest of banknote counterfeit members.”

The Chosun Jeongpansa Company counterfeiting case became the turning point in the situation of government in liberation. The US Military Government, which has been taking a conciliatory gesture toward the Communist Party, started to press the Communist Party on the occasion of this incident.The public’s gaze on the Communist Party has also become colder which committed a civilian crime that disturbed the national economy by counterfeiting the bills.

The left-right wing joint merging matter and the new tactical matter were succeeded to secret trip to Moscow by three persons Kim Il-sung, Park Hun-young, and Huh Ga-yi who were under fourth secret meeting during June 27th～July 12th.

"300만 원 이상의 위조 지폐로써
남조선 일대를 교란하던
지폐 위조단 일당이 일망타진되었다.
지폐 위조단에는 조선공산당 간부 2명
조선정판사에 근무하는 조선공산당원 14명이 관련되었다.
지폐 위조단의 소굴인 해방일보를 인쇄하는
조선정판사 소재지 근택近澤 빌딩은
조선공산당 본부이다."

조선정판사 위폐 사건은 해방 정국의 분수령이었네
그 동안 공산당에 대해 유화적 태도를 취하던 미 군정청은
이 사건을 계기로 공산당을 압박하기 시작했네

지폐를 위조해 경제를 교란하는 민생 범죄를 저지른
공산당을 바라보는 국민의 시선도 싸늘해졌네

좌우 합작 문제와 신전술 문제는
제4차 비밀 회동(1946. 06. 27.~07. 12.) 중이던
김일성, 박헌영, 허가이許哥而 3인의
모스크바 밀행으로 이어졌네

Park Hun-young and Kim Il-sung accompanied by Huh Sung-taek, Lee Tae-joon, Park Chi-woo discussed intensively holding the fifth secret meeting twice during 16th～22nd of July. In the meeting of the standing committee of the Organizing Committee of the Communist Party of North Korea, they discussed on unifying three parties of Communist Party of Korea, South Korean Shinmindang Party and Korea People's Party, and the counterfeiting matter of Chosun Jeongpansa Company, establishing sole government, left-right wing unifying matter and 'new tactics for self-defense' matter were discussed intensively.

Park Hun-young refrained from direct criticizing or hostile action to the US military, ordered active struggle and physical resistance through 'new tactics'.

The core of the new tactics was dual tactics to use 'Offensive pressing tactics' for the US military and to use "Self-defense tactics" against the right wing forces in South Korea.

On the occasion of the counterfeiting case of Chosun Jeongpansa Company, the U.S. Military Government's all-round pressure was continued.

The arrest warrant was issued to Park Hun-young, Lee Gang-guk and others.

Park Hun-young escaped to North Korea hidden inside the coffin disguised as dead by way of funeral procession on the 5th of September.

허성택, 이태준, 박치우를 대동한 박헌영과 김일성의
제5차 비밀 회동 (1946. 07. 16.~22.)은 두 차례에 걸친
북조선공산당 조직위원회, 상무위원회 회의를 통해
3당 합당(조선공산당, 남조선신민당, 조선인민당)과
조선정판사 위폐 사건, 그리고 단독 정부 수립과
좌우 합작 문제, '정당 방위에 의한 신전술' 등이
집중적으로 논의되었네

미 군정에 대해 직접적 비난이나 적대 행위를 자제하고
'신전술新戰術' 을 통하여 적극적인 투쟁과 물리적 저항을
박헌영은 지시했네 「註釋*35」

미 군정에 대해서는 '공세적 압박 전술' 을
남한 내 우익 세력에 대해서는 '정당 방위적인 자위 전술' 로
대응하는 이중 전술이 신전술의 핵심이었네

조선정판사 위폐 사건을 계기로 좌익 세력에 대한
미 군정청의 전방위적인 압박이 계속되었네

박헌영, 이강국 등에 대해 체포 영장을 발부하자
관 속의 시체로 위장한 박헌영은
영구차 행렬로 북한으로 탈출했네(1946. 09. 05.) 「註釋*36」

The US Military Government classified the political powers of South Korea around May 1946;
Rhee Syng-man and Kim Gu as extreme rightist, Kim Kyu-sik and Won Se-hun as mid rightist, Yeo Wun-hyung as mid leftist and Park Hun-young as extreme leftist power.

The US Military Government separated the left-wing camp into mid leftist and extreme leftistand isolated the extreme leftist and pursued policies to lead the country mixed by mid leftist Yeo Wun-hyung and rightists but there was a subtle difference between the US State Department.

The US State Department wished to organize the political power for the benefit of the United States with the mid leftist and mid rightist getting rid of both extreme leftist and rightist. Meanwhile the US Military Government wished to isolate the extreme leftist and weaken the leftist camp owing to the power of both mid leftist and mid rightist.

After three rounds of meetings by Kim Kyu-sik, Won Se-hoon, Yeo Wun-hyung and Hwang Jin-nam on the 25th May and 30th May and the 14th June by the arrangement of advisor lieutenant Bertsch of the US Military Government, a statement was announced by lieutenant general Hodge in relation with the start of the joint movement, and left and right wing representatives were decided on the 19th of July.

미 군정은 남한의 정치 세력을 이승만, 김구 중심의 극우 세력
김규식, 원세훈 등의 중도 우파 세력
여운형 중심의 중도 좌파 세력
박헌영 중심의 극좌 세력으로 분류하고 있었네(1946. 05.)

미 군정은 좌익 진영을 극좌와 중도 좌파로 분리하여
극좌 세력은 고립시키고, 여운형 중심의 중도 좌파와 합작
우익이 정국을 주도할 수 있도록 정책을 추진하고 있었으나
국무부와는 미묘한 시각 차이를 드러냈네

국무부는 극좌와 함께 극우 세력도 배제한
중도의 좌, 우 세력을 중심으로
미국의 이익에 부합한 정치 세력을 구성하고자 하였고
미 군정은 극좌 세력만을 고립화 함으로
중도의 좌, 우 세력 합작을 통한 좌익 진영의 약화를 시도했네

미 군정 고문 버치(Bertsch, L.) 중위의 주선으로
김규식金奎植과 원세훈元世勳, 여운형呂運亨과 황진남黃鎭南의
3차례의 회동(05. 25. / 05. 30. / 06. 14.)을 거친 후
합작 운동 개시에 관한 하지 중장의 성명이 나오면서
좌, 우 세력의 대표가 결정되었네(1946. 07. 19.)

The right-wing representatives were president Kim Kyu-sik, representatives Won Se-hoon, Kim Bong-joon, An Jae-hong and Choi Dong-o, and the left-wing representatives were president Yeo Woon-hyung, representatives Huh Hun, Chung No-sik, Lee Gang-gook, and Sung Ju-sik.

The both camp delegates held two round preliminary talks through July 22nd-25th, for regular meetings, and inaugurated the Left and Right-wing Joint Committee on the 26th of July.

The first regular meeting of the Left and Right-wing Joint Committee was held on the 26th of July but it resulted to show serious conflict between the two camps on the merging principle.

The left-wing camp supported the three foreign ministers meeting in Moscow with the 5 articles for the merging principle:
To open the US-Soviet Joint Committee again, the land reform by confiscating the land from land owners with no payments and distribute them to the people free of charge. Nationalizing the important businesses, and completing the basic tasks of democracy.

To getting rid of the pro-Japanese head betrayers, and “fascist betrayers’ and eradication of the terrorists and to release the arrested and imprisoned democratic patriots immediately. To transfer the government to the People’s Committee opposing the creation of a Military Advisory Organization and Legislative Organization.

우측 대표는 주석 김규식, 원세훈, 김봉준, 안재홍, 최동오
좌측 대표는 주석 여운형, 허헌, 정노식, 이강국, 성주식이었네

양측 대표들은 정례 회의를 위한
두 차례 예비 회담(07. 22.～25.)을 거치면서
좌우합작위원회를 발족시켰네(1946. 07. 25.)「註釋*37」

좌우합작위원회는 1차 회담(1946. 07. 26.)부터
합작 원칙을 둘러싸고 심각한 갈등을 드러냈네

좌익 진영이 주장한 합작 원칙 5개 조항은
모스크바 삼상 회의 결정 지지와 미소공동위원회 속개
무상 몰수 무상 분배의 토지 개혁과 중요 사업 국유화
친일파 민족 반역자 친 '파쇼 반동' 거두 배제와
테러 박멸 검거 투옥된 민주 애국 지사의 석방
인민위원회로 정권 이양과 군정 고문 기관
입법 기관 창설 반대 등이었네

우익 진영의 합작 원칙은 신탁 문제는
임시 정부 수립 한 후에 미소공동위원회와 협의하여
자주 독립 정신에 근거하여 해결할 것
정치, 경제, 교육의 모든 제도 법령은
균등 사회 건설을 목표로 하여 국민대표회의에서 결정할 것

The principle of right-wing merging was that trusteeship matter is to be solved based on the spirit of self-independence discussing with the US-Soviet Joint Committee, and decide all the matters of politics, economics, education etc. at the People's Representative Committee with purpose of establishing a non-biased society. With regard to the castigating matter of the pro-Japanese betrayers, it will be dealt by composing the special court after the establishment of Provisional Government.

The Left and Right-wing Merging Committee was stalemated due to unavailability of narrowing the different opinion, Yeo Wun-hyung announced his opinion actively after his returning from Pyongyang having 4th secret meeting with Kim Il-sung during 23rd～30th September;

To establish the Provisional Government for democracy through left and right-wing bilateral merging according to the decision of the three foreign ministers meeting in Moscow, and to announce a joint statement requesting the resumption of the US-Soviet Joint Committee, to establish local autonomy on the basis of social labor laws and political freedom and to implement the land reform, nationalization of important industries, to promote the ordinances to deal with pro-Japanese national traitors, to release the North and South Korean politicians, and to try to stop "terror" actions of North and South. Organizing the legislative organization and to try to plan an operational plan, and the absolute guarantee of freedom of press and media, assembly, association, publication, transportation, and voting etc.

친일파 민족 반역자는 징치를 하되
임시 정부 수립 후, 특별 법정을 구성하여 처리할 것 등이었네

견해 차이를 좁히지 못해 지지부진하던 좌우합작위원회는
평양에서 김일성과 4차 비밀 회동(09. 23.~30.)을 하고
돌아온 여운형이 적극적으로 의견을 개진함으로써
7개 항의 합작 원칙이 결정되었네(1946. 10. 04.)

모스크바 삼상 회의 결정에 따라
남과 북의 좌우 합작으로 민주주의 임시 정부를 수립할 것
미소공동위원회 속개를 요청하는 공동 성명을 발표할 것

토지 개혁 실시, 중요 산업 국유화 및
사회, 노동법령 및 정치적 자유를
기반으로 지방 자치제를 확립할 것

친일파, 민족 반역자를 처리할 조례 추진과
남북 정치인 석방 및 남북 좌우의 '테러' 행동 제지 노력

그리고 입법 기구 구성과 운영 방안 모색과
언론, 집회, 결사, 출판, 교통, 투표 자유의 절대 보장 등이었네

As Korea got liberation, South Korea suffered the short of electricity stopped by the North due to the division of North and South where Japanese capital and technicians evacuated, and due to the flooding population of overseas returnees and displaced people from North Korea, the lives of workers and farmers living in South Korea were in a more deprived condition than under the Japanese colonial rule.

The character of September struggle of the Communist Party of Korea which simulated massive strike struggle (new strategy) exploiting economic conditions such as food shortages, unemployment, and index price hike etc. initiated with railway labor union's strike was spread nationwide under the leadership of the National Council of the Korean Trade Unions. It was changed from an economic struggle to a political struggle.

There were signs of their becoming terrorists as the railway strike spreads nationwide, the US Military Government mobilized 3,000 police officers on the 30th of September and arrested one thousand railroad workers who were in sit-down strike.

Although the Seoul Struggle Committee was closed by the police and the Korean Confederation of Trade Unions and right-wing youth organization, the massive strike occurred in Daegu on the 1st of October in protest against the food policy of the US Military Government triggered to October struggle and continued till middle of December.

해방이 되자 일본의 자본과 기술자가 철수한 남한은
남북 분단으로 북한에서 오던 송전이 두절되고
해외 귀환자나 월남 실향민 등으로 인한 인구 급증으로
남한에 거주하는 노동자, 농민들의 생활은
일제 강점기보다 더한 궁핍한 상태에 놓였네

식량난과 실업, 물가 상승 등의 경제 상황을 교묘히 이용하여
대규모 파업 투쟁(신전략)을 선동한
조선공산당의 9월 투쟁은 철도노동조합으로 시작하여
조선노동조합전국평의회(전평) 주도 하에
전국적으로 확산되면서
경제적 투쟁에서 정치적 투쟁으로 성격이 바뀌고 있었네

철도 파업이 확산되면서 폭동화될 조짐을 보이자
미 군정은(1946. 09. 30.) 경찰관 3천 명을 동원하여
농성 중인 철도 노동자 1천 명을 검거했네

경찰과 대한노총, 우익 청년 단체에 의해
전평의 서울투쟁위원회는 폐쇄되었으나
미 군정의 식량 정책에 항의하여
대구에서 발생한 대규모 시위는(1946. 10. 01.)
10월 항쟁으로 번져 12월 중순까지 계속되었네 「註釋*38」

The North Korean Labor Party was inaugurated by the participation of the North Korean Communist Party in the party convention with the Korean New Democratic Party during 28th～30th of August, Yeo Wun-hyung, president of the Korean Communist Party and Paik Nam-hun,
the president of the South Korea New Democratic Party started to maneuver to make one unified party with the three parties in order to enforce the South Korean leftists.

The three parties' merging Preparatory Committee Meeting was held on the 4th of September.
They adopted three parties' decision and declaration, and the code of the merging.
The South Korean Labor Party Preparatory Committee established the south korea labor party by the negotiation between the extreme merge pursuing members and reasonable merge pursuing members.
At the end of the negotiations, they organized the South Korean Labor Party on the 23rd of November.

In the October struggle following the September struggle, the Communist Party of Korea actively participated in the struggle and leaded the political situation with the merged three parties.
But the left and right wing merge movement lost its power and went bankrupt when the formation of a transitional legislator become in detail by the US Military Government.

북조선공산당이 조선신민당과
합당 대회(08. 28.～30.)를 통하여
북조선노동당을 창립하자
남한의 좌익 세력의 결집을 위하여 조선공산당은
여운형이 당수로 있던 조선인민당朝鮮人民黨과
백남운白南雲이 당수로 있던 남조선신민당南朝鮮新民黨의
3당 합당 공작에 착수했네

9월 4일, 3당 합당 준비 위원회 연석회의 개최
3당 합당 결정서와 선언 및 강령이 채택하고
남조선노동당준비위원회를 구성하고
급진적 합당 추진파와 합리적 합당 추진파는 협의 끝에
남조선노동당을 창당하였네(1946. 11. 23.) 「註釋*39」

9월 투쟁에 이어서 10월 항쟁에도 적극적으로
개입한 조선공산당이 3당 합당으로 정국을 주도하고
미 군정의 과도 입법 의원 창설이 구체화되자
좌우 합작 운동은 동력을 상실한 채 파산하였네

미 군정장관 러치(Lerche, A. L.)는
조선 인민이 요구하는 법령을
조선 인민의 손으로 제정하는 입법 기관의 창설을
미군 사령관 하지 중장에게 건의하여

Lerche A. L., US Secretary of Defense requested the creation of the laws required by the Korea people, and asked to J. R. Hodge, the commander of US military to authorize the provisional government of the Republic of Korea to establish a legislative body enacted by the hands of the Korean people.
"The Act on the Establishment of a Transitional Parliamentary Legislative Members of Korea" was declared as military code on the 24th of August.

US Military Government insisted on the reason why establishing the legislative institutions was they would like to train Koreans to acquire practical skills such as drafting laws and regulations with intention to confirm the superiority of the democratic system responding to the North Korean regime under the Soviet rule.

When general Hodge saw the 45 persons one by one of who were elected by indirect elections during the 21st～31st October, Rhee Syng-man was seemed to be taking over the transitional legislator, and general Hodge asked Kim Kyu-sik for a list of 45 members elected by the administration.

The South Korean transitional legislators were scheduled to be in the opening on the 4th of November.
There was a request of reelection by the left and right wing merged joint committee pointing out that there were problems of irregularity in the election and pro-Japanese matters, and this request was admitted. Reelection was held to elect legislators from Seoul and Gangwon Province but the same candidates were re-elected.

「조선과도입법의원의 창설에 관한 법령」을
군정법령으로 공포하였네(1946. 08. 24.)

미 군정은 입법 기관 설치 이유에 대해
한국인에게 민주주의 제도를 훈련시키고
법령 초안 작성 등의 실무 기술을 익히게 함으로써
소련 지배하의 북한 체제에 대응, 민주주의 체제의 우월성을
확인시키려는 의도라고 주장했네

간접 선거(1946. 10. 21.~31.)로 선출된
과도입법 민선 의원 45명의 면면을 볼 때
이승만이 과도 입법 의원을 장악할 것으로 보이자
하지는 관선 의원 45명의 명단을 김규식에게 요청했네

11월 4일, 개원이 예정이었던
남조선과도입법의원은 「**註釋*40**」
선거의 부정과 친일 인사 문제 등을 지적한
좌우합작위원회의 요구가 관철되자
서울과 강원도의 입법 의원 선출을 위해
재선거를 실시하였으나 동일한 후보가 다시 선출되었네

하지는 해방 전 수년간 일본에게 부역했다는 이유를 내세워
김성수를 포함한 3명의 민선 입법 위원의 자격을 박탈했네

General Hodge deprived three legislative members including Kim Sung-soo who were elected by the people on account of they served as collaborators to Japan for many years before liberation.

In the preliminary talks on the 11th of December, representatives from the Korea Democratic Party were dissatisfied with the reelection of Seoul and Gangwon-do and refused to register, and failed to meet the quorum three quarters of the total which was defined in the bill.

The US Military Government promulgated the amendment of the bill immediately after constituting a quorum with one-half of the total members, and at the preliminary meeting of that day Kim Kyu-sik was elected as chairman with the absolute majority of 49 votes among 53.
And then they adopted a resolution against the trusteeship but only one person Ahn Jae-hong opposed to it.

General Hodge newly established Korean Affairs Department under the guidance of the US Military Government and appointed An Jae-hong as the person in charge.

The conservatives were Rhee Syng-man who was chosen by election and the Council of Independence Promotion line members while the representatives appointed by lieutenant general Hodge, selected by administration were mostly left and right-wing merged members. Yeo Wun-hyung quit the position of transitional legislative representative on account of the irregularities in the election.

11일의 예비 회담에서 한민당 출신 의원들이
서울시와 강원도의 재선거에 대한 불만을 표시하고
등원을 거부하자 법령에 규정한
회의 구성의 정족수(전체 의원의 4분의 3)가 미달되었네

미 군정은 즉시 전체 의원의 2분의 1로
정족수를 구성하는 수정 법안을 공포하여
예비 회의에서 참석 의원 53명 중
49표의 절대 다수로 김규식이 의장으로 당선되었네
이어서 신탁 통치 반대 결의안을 체택하였는데
반대자는 안재홍 의원 한 사람뿐이었네

미 군정의 지침 아래 한국 관련 업무를 신설한
미 군정 장관은 그 자리에 안재홍을 임명했네

선거로 선출된 과도 민선 입법의원은
이승만李承晩의 독립촉성국민회 계열 등 보수 세력이
하지 중장이 임명한 관선 의원에는 좌우 합작파가 다수였네
여운형은 선거 부정을 이유로 과도 입법 의원을 탈퇴했네

과도 입법 의원은 한국의 최초 대의 정치 기관이었네

The transitional legislative institution was the Korea's first representative political organization.

Although these enacted laws and ordinances shall be effective only with the consent of the minister of the transitional legislative body, it was meaningful that the South Korean transitional government could have the form of division of powers, namely, the administration, legislation and judiciary.

When the Republicans won in the election of the United States, Rhee Syng-man made his mind to visit US saying "My intimate friends are Republicans. Hodge is a member of Democrats. However, today Republicans got political power"

General Hodge got angry with Rhee Syng-man who was trying to contact Washington without a word of consultation with him as Rhee Syng-man tried to protest officially with regard to the policies and programs which were implemented in Korea.

On his way to the United States, he stayed two days in Tokyo during the 4th～5th of December.

In an interview with MacArthur, Rhee Syng-man accused that supporting the neutrals is supporting the communists and it should be retreated.

General Hodge visited US around middle of February 1947 said something like he considerably agreed with Rhee Syng-man's opinion on the situation and prospects. However he couldn't easily forget the past

제정한 법령은 군정장관의 동의를 얻어야만
효력이 발생하는 과도 입법 기관이지만
행정부, 사법부와 함께 남조선과도정부가
삼권 분립의 형태를 갖추게 하였다는 데
그 의의가 있었네

11월 5일 미국 국회 의원 선거에서 공화당이 승리했네

"미국의 나와 친한 친구들은 공화당원이다.
 하지는 민주당원이다.
 그러나 이제 공화당이 정권을 장악했다."
고 말한 이승만은 미국 방문을 결심했네

자신과 한 마디 상의 없이
워싱턴과 접촉을 하려고 하는 이승만에게
하지 장군은 분노했네

미국으로 가는 도중
도쿄東京에 이틀(12. 04~05.)을 머문 이승만은
맥아더(Douglas MacArthur)와의 면담에서
하지의 중간파 지원을 용공 정책이라 비난하면서
이를 철회시키라고 주장했네

sediment for Rhee Syng-man.

On March 2, 1947, when Rhee Syng-man was making a trip to US, Kim Gu convened an urgent meeting of the Korean National People's Congress composed of 1,500 delegates and asked to approve the establishment of the Provisional Government of the Republic of Korea.

The Korean National People's Congress carefully discussed Kim Gu's request for the expansion and strengthening the provisional government to declare immediately the sovereignty of Korea.
As a result of careful discussion, they recommended Rhee Syng-man as its president and Kim Gu as deputy president. (Article of Dong A Ilbo daily newspaper on March 5, 1947)

Kim Gu and his supporters were angry at the denial of the Korean National People's Congress for the planning of the proclamation of the provisional government. But Kim Kyu-sik and other neutral persons thought that the North and South coalition government was the only way to unify Korea.

Owing to the decision of the Korean National People's Congress, the confrontation between the Provisional Government and the US Military

1947년 2월 중순, 미국을 방문한 하지 장군은
남조선의 상황과 전망에 대해 상당한 인식을
이승만과 공유한 것처럼 말은 했지만
이승만에 대한 앙금은 쉽게 지울 수가 없었네

이승만이 미국을 방문하고 있던
1947년 3월 2일, 대의원 1,500명으로 구성된
한국국민대표회의를 긴급 소집한 김구는
대한민국 임시 정부의 수립 승인을
한국국민대표회의에 요청했네

한국국민대표회의는
한국의 자주권을 즉각 선언해 달라는
임시 정부의 확대 강화에 대한
김구의 요청을 신중히 토의한 결과
임시 정부 주석에 이승만을, 부주석에 김구를 추대했네
(1947. 03. 05. 동아일보 기사)

김구와 그 지지자들은 임시 정부의 선포 계획을
국민대표회의가 부결시킨 데 대하여 분노했네
김규식을 위시한 중도 노선 인사들은 남북 연립 정부가
한국을 통일할 수 있는 유일한 길이라고 생각했네

Government could be avoided. Rhee Syng-man could change the Provisional Government into political party instead of opposing power although Kim Gu's intention was different.

After the World War II, when the United States and the Soviet Union were struggling for a balance of power, the United Kingdom announced to the Mediterranean countries such as Turkey and Greece that it can no longer afford to provide its aid.

As these countries were risk of being placed under the influence of the Soviet Union, president Truman asked the Congress for $400 million to fight against the expansion policy of the Communists on the 12th of March.

This policy was known as "The Truman Doctrine for Greece and Turkey" which ended with a post-war effort of US to build peace in cooperation with the Soviet Union, and it meant a change in US foreign policy to pursue peace and stability by countering communist imperialism in the future.

Rhee Syng-man left the United States after four months of visiting the United States on the 5th of April visited Tokyo and Taiwan to meet MacArthur and Jiang Jieshi. Rhee Syng-man repatriated together with Lee Chung-chun (Jee Chung-chun) who was a Commander of the Liberation Army by Jiang Jieshi's private plane on the 21st of April.

국민대표회의 결정으로 임시 정부와 미 군정의 대립은
피할 수가 있었으며 이승만은 김구의 의도와는 달리
임정을 저항 세력이 아닌 정치 정당으로 바꿀 수 있었네

제2차 세계 대전이 끝난 후
미국과 소련이 세력 균형을 이루기 위해 투쟁을 벌이고 있을 때
영국은 터키, 그리스 등 지중해 국가들에게
더 이상 원조를 제공할 여력이 없다고 발표했네
이들 국가가 소련의 영향권 내에 놓일 위험에 처하자
트루먼(Harry S. Truman)은 공산주의자들의 팽창 정책에
맞서 싸우기 위하여 의회에 4억 달러를 요청했네(1947. 03. 12.)

'그리스와 터키에 대한 트루먼 독트린' 으로 알려진
이 정책은 소련과 협력하여 평화를 구축하려는 미국의
전후의 노력은 끝났으며 공산 제국주의에 대항함으로써
평화와 안정을 추구하겠다는
미국의 대외 정책 변화를 의미한 것이었네 「註釋*41」

4개월 간의 미국 방문을 끝내고
미국을 떠난(1947. 04. 05.) 이승만은 도쿄와 타이완에 들러
맥아더와 장제스와 만난 후 장제스의 전용기 편으로
광복군 사령관 이청천(지청천)과 함께 귀국했네(1947. 04. 21.)

Rhee Syng-man's successful result of visiting US was announcement of the Truman Doctrine and the discussion of large-scale US economic aid to South Korea. Two days after his returning home on the 23rd of April, Rhee Syng-man declared a public statement.

"We appreciate that our overseas activities were helped a lot as a result of the nationwide support of Korean people. The most remarkable thing that I spoke in the United States was that even after a year and half after liberation, we are under the management of the Military Government without having independent government and we are suffering from hardships and difficulties in resolving international issues. We need to establish self-independent government and all the occupied countries in the East and the West organized their governments by conducting general elections.

Even Japan which was a defeated nation established the government in a general election.

But we declared that we had so far been under the management of the Military Government which is unfair fact and that whole of our nation is determined not to wait any more.

And the US authorities concerned and all public opinion began to admit our claim" As internal and external pressure was increased due to the delayed process of Korean issues such as an establishment of an independent nation, they started to make an effort to resume the US and Soviet Joint Committee.

The second US and Soviet Joint Committee was resumed on May 21, 1947 through long time negotiation by means of letters between General

트루먼 독트린의 발표와 미국의 대규모 경제 원조 논의가
이승만의 미국 방문 성과였네
귀국 이틀 후(04. 23.) 이승만은 대 국민 성명서를 발표했네

"그 동안에 국내 동포들이 전국적으로 후원하신 결과로
우리의 해외 활동에 많은 도움이 된 것을 감사합니다.
내가 미국에 가서 가장 역설한 바는 해방 후 1년 반이 지나도록
한인의 독립 정부가 없이 군정청 관리 하에서
민생 곤란과 국제상 중요 문제의 해결책이 없이
고통을 받고 있는 중이니
하루 바삐 자치 자주하는 정부 수립이 필요하며,
따라서 동서양 모든 점령국이 다 총선거를 행하여
정부를 조직하였고,
심지어 전패국인 일본까지 총선거로써 정부를 수립하였는데
우리는 지금까지 군정 관리를 받게 됨은
사실상으로도 불공평함이니 우리 민족 전체는
무슨 방식으로서든지 더 기다리지 않을 결심이란 것을
선언한 바 미국의 당국과 모든 공론이 모두
우리의 주장을 옳게 시인하기에 이른 것입니다."

독립 국가 수립 등 한국 문제 처리가 지연되면서
내외적 압력이 높아지자
미국과 소련의 미소공동위원회의 재개를 위한 노력이 시작됐네

Hodge and General Chischakov, and the letter of Marshall G. C., US Secretary of State Department and Molotov V. M., foreign minister of Soviet Union.

As the second US and Soviet Joint Committee was resumed, general Hodge warned that the Moscow Agreement on Trusteeship must be observed, and as a way to constrain the activities of Rhee Syng-man, they removed Rhee's house phone and kept weekly censorship of post mails and stopped all means of contact with the people including radio talks.

There were no Koreans in the conference hall where to decide the future of Korea. tried to determine our destiny regardless of our opinion in accordance with their political, economic and strategic interests.

At their own meeting without Korean person's participation, they tried to set a rule for the kind of Koreans who will participate in the conference and type of speech that will determine the fate of Korea.

They were doing arrogant dictatorship in the name of democracy with already made decision that the form of future government need to be a "coalition".

They tried to decide how to procure people who will take the position of "government form" they impose through the meetings.

하지 중장과 치스차코프 대장 사이의 서신, 미 국무장관
마샬과 소련 외상 몰로토프의 서신을 통한 교섭 끝에
제2차 미소공동위원회가 재개되었네(1947. 05. 21.)

제2차 미소공동위원회가 재개되자 하지 장군은
신탁 통치에 관한 모스크바 협정은 반드시 준수되어야
한다는 경고와 함께 회의 기간 중 이승만의 활동을
제약하기 위한 방법으로 이승만의 자택 전화기를 철거하고
우편물 검열과 함께 매주 해 오던 라디오 담화 등
국민과 접촉하는 모든 수단을 중단시켰네

한국의 미래를 결정하는 회의장에 한국인은 없었네.
우리의 의사와는 상관없이
정치적 · 경제적 · 전략적 이익에 따라
우리의 운명을 결정하려고 했네

한국인의 참여 없는 그들만의 회의에서
한국의 운명을 좌우하는 회의에 참여할 한국인의 부류와
발언의 종류에 대한 규칙을 정하려 했네

앞으로 수립될 정부의 형태가
'연립' 형태가 되어야 한다는 결정을 내려놓고
민주주의라는 이름으로 오만한 독재를 하고 있었네

It meant that they would discuss the matters with us in accordance with the results after selling the freedom of choice of our country.

They forced the trusteeship under the disguised friendship to 95% of the 30 million Korean people who love peace and against trusteeship even with their death.

They diluted, distorted, and altered the true meaning of "trusteeship" and demanded a guarantee that they will not modify even their plausible interpretations of its meaning and insisted that it should be considered from a "broader" global point of view through the relationship with Soviet Union so far as Korean matter is concerned.

In addition to the active leftists and neutrals and even a part of rightists such as Korea Democratic Party decided to participate in the meeting by declaring their position "In order to establish a unified government, participation in the Joint Committee has become inevitable and the trusteeship matter should be opposed by the total national opinion after the establishment of the Provisional Government".

Almost all political parties and social organizations submitted petitions for the participation in the Joint Committee except Rhee Syng-man and Kim Gu.

그들은 그들이 강요하는 '정부 형태' 의 보직을
채울 인사들을 조달하는 방법을 회의를 통해
결정하려고 했네
나라의 선택 자유를 팔아넘긴 후에
결과에 따른 문제만을 우리와 협의를 하겠다는 의미였네

이들은 친구라는 가면을 쓰고
3천만 명의 평화를 사랑하는 국민 중 95%가
결사 반대하고 있는 신탁 통치를 강요했네

'신탁 통치' 의 참된 의미를 희석하고 왜곡하고 변조하더니
그럴 듯한 해석조차도 수정하지 않겠다는 보장을 요구하자
한국 문제는 소련과의 관계를 통해 '보다 넓은'
세계적인 관점에서 고려되어야 한다는 주장을 했네

미소공동위원회에 적극적인 좌익계와 중간파 외에도
한민당韓民黨 등 일부 우익 진영에서도
"통일 정부 수립을 위하여
 공동 위원회 참가는 불가피하게 되었으며
 신탁 문제는 임정 수립 뒤 민족총의로 반대해야 한다."
는 입장을 밝히며 공동위원회 참가를 결정했네

이승만과 김구를 제외한

The number of political parties and social organizations in South Korea that submitted petitions to the Joint Committee was 425 and those of North Korea was 36, and the number of members was 70 million.

Although there was a strange circumstance that the number of the members was doubled the whole population, the joint meeting with South Korean political parties and social organizations was held in Seoul on the 25th June as planned by the representatives of the US-Soviet Joint Committee. They moved to Pyongyang to hold general meeting from the 30th June, they had a joint meeting with North Korean political parties and social organizations on the 1st of July.

Yeo Wun-hyung returned to the political party before the second round US-Soviet Joint Committee was shot to death on the 19th July at the Hyehwa-dong intersection by a terrorist who attacked him by rushing into the running car.

Yeo Wun-hyung was disturbed by the small and large scale terrorists ever since the first terrorist attack but he could not avoid the 12th terror.

Han Ji-keun was arrested at the home of Han Hyun-woo who assassinated Song Jin-wuinteracted with the people involved in the 'Gyokmong Euisook'.

These persons contacted with Yang Geun-hwan of the "Innovation Detective Club"

거의 모든 정당, 사회 단체가 공위 참가 청원서를 제출했네

공동위원회에 청원서를 제출한
남한의 정당, 사회 단체 수는 425개
북한의 정당, 사회 단체 수는 36개이며
회원 수는 7,000만 명이었네

당시 인구의 두 배나 되는 기이한 상황이 벌어졌지만
공동위원회의 미소 대표들은 남한의 정당 및
사회 단체와 합동 회의를 서울에서 가졌고(1947. 06. 25.)
평양으로 옮겨서 본회의를 개최하면서
북한의 정당 및 사회 단체와 합동 회의(1947. 07. 01.)를 가졌네

제2차 미소공동위원회를 앞두고 정계에 복귀한 여운형은
7월 19일, 혜화동 로터리에서 달리는 차 안으로 난입한
괴한에 의해 총격을 받고 암살당했네

첫 번째 테러 발생 이후 끊임없이 크고 작은 테러에
시달렸던 여운형은 12번째 테러를 끝내 피하지 못했네

체포된 한지근은 송진우 암살범 한현우韓賢宇의 집에서
'격몽의숙擊蒙義塾'「**註釋*42**」관련자들과 교류했네

and Yeom-Dong-jin of 'Baek Euisa' and they tried to find the subject of terror.

They assumed that Yeo Wun-hyung was responsible for the division of the people and decided to remove him.

Han Ji-keun could be waived death sentence because of being a minor, and was kidnapped by the North Korean soldiers during the Korean War but his life was unknown thereafter.

The second US-Soviet Joint Committee seemed making progress, but it was deadlocked again over the issues of discussion.

They could not overcome the conflicts of the First Joint Committee between the Soviet's 'Strong support of the decision of the three foreign ministerial talks' and US 'freedom of expressing opinion'. In the mid-August, the US Military Government carried out the massive arrest of the Namrodang Party members and left-wing figures on account of their illegal destructive activities, the meeting was broken down.

이들은 당시 극우 테러리스트로 활동하고 있었던
'혁신탐정단' 의 양근환梁謹煥, '백의사' 의 염동진廉東鎭
등과 접촉, 테러 대상을 찾다가
여운형을 민족 분열에 책임이 있다고 단정하고
그를 제거하기로 결심했네 「註釋*43」

미성년자라는 이유로 사형을 면한 한지근은

한국 전쟁 때 북한군에 의해 끌려간 뒤
그의 생사는 알려진 바 없네

진전을 보이던 제2차 미소공동위원회는
협의 대상 문제를 둘러싸고 또다시 교착 상태에 빠졌네

소련 측의 '삼국 외상 회의 결정 고수' 와
미국 측의 '의사 표시의 자유' 라는 갈등을 극복하지 못한
제1차 공동위원회는 불법 파괴 활동을 자행한다는 이유로
8월 중순 미군정이 남로당 및 좌익계 인사들의
대대적인 검거를 시작하면서 결렬되었네

소련 측 대표 스티코프가
"모스크바 3상 회의 결정과 공위 업무를 지지해 온
 남한의 좌익 인사의 탄압은

Soviet representative Stikov vigorously protested saying that "The oppression of the South Korea's left wing that supported the decision of the Moscow three foreign ministers meeting and Joint Committee's affairs was a hindrance to the Joint Committee project". The US representative Brown W.G. rather requested to release Cho Man-sik who was imprisoned in North Korea protesting that it is "Interference in South Korea's internal affairs."

To regret the mistake and to fix the mistake, and to take initiative in insisting that the international treaty was the first thing to be abolished was a totally separate matter.

공동위원회 사업을 방해하는 처사"
라고 강경하게 항의하자, 미국 측 대표 브라운(Brown. W. G.)은
"남한 내정에 간섭하는 것"
이라고 반박하며 오히려 북한에 감금되어 있는
조만식을 석방하라고 요구했네

실수를 후회하는 일과 그 실수를 고치기 위해
국제 협약 폐기를 앞장서서 주장하는 일은
전혀 별개의 사안이었네

The cold war has already begun

It was a dilemma for US policymakers to have a fear of probable provoking a disaster if the US discards the agreement first with the Soviet Union.

When the second US-Soviet Joint Committee was broken down, Chang Duk-soo thought that there would be nothing more to expect about the US-Soviet Joint Committee and judged that he should appeal to the United Nations to conduct a general election. And he went to the US special envoy, Wade Meyer and insisted the inevitability of establishing a sole government in South Korea in September 1947.

Marshall, the US Secretary of State assumed that there was no result in the efforts of US-Soviet Joint Committee for the past two years and announced statement on the 17th of September "As the Korean issue is presented to the General Assembly of the United Nations, I hope that measures will be taken to make Korea independent instead of ruling by trusteeship", and US transferred this issue to the United Nations.

Vyshinskii, A.Y., the Soviet chief representative of the United Nations General Assembly opposed it strongly saying "It's a direct violation of the agreement between US and Soviet to propose Korean issue to the UN. However, Marshall's proposal was passed by the Steering Committee of the United Nations General Assembly on the 21st of September.

냉전은 이미 시작되었고

미국이 먼저 소련과의 협약을 폐기한다면
재앙과 같은 결과를 초래할 줄 모른다는 두려움이
미국의 정책 당국자가 갖고 있는 딜레마였네

제2차 미소공동위원회가 결렬되자
'미소공동위원회에 대해 더는 기대할 것이 없다.' 고
생각한 장덕수는 국제연합(UN)에 호소해
총선거를 실시해야 한다고 판단하고
김성수와 함께 미국 특사 웨드마이어를 찾아가서
남한만의 단독 정부 수립의 불가피성을
주장했네(1947. 09.)

미 국무장관 마샬은 2년 동안의 미소공동위원회의 노력이
성과가 없었음을 전제로

"한국 문제가 국제연합 총회에 상정됨에 따라
 신탁 통치를 거치지 않고
 한국을 독립시키는 수단이 강구되기를 바란다."
는 성명(1947. 09. 17.)과 함께 미국은 한국 문제를

Lieutenant general Brown, the chief US representative proposed to stop the work of the Joint Committee until the discussion on the Korean issue over at the 62nd plenary session on the 18th of October.

Stevkov, the chief representative of the Soviet Union, announced the withdrawal of the Soviet delegation from Seoul and left Seoul with more than 50 Soviet delegations for Pyongyang and the 2nd US-Soviet Joint Committee was closed on the 21st of October.

Kim Gu could be successful to get the consent of Rhee Syng-man in November by demanding the unity of right-wing people with the support of National Assembly instead of cooperating with Rhee Syng-man's route. However, on the occasion of the assassination of Chang Duk-soo on the 2nd of December, the unity of Kim Gu, Rhee Syng-man, and the Korea Democratic Party was finished in failure.

Chang Duk-soo was shot to death by five gunners of Park Kwang-ok who was a current policeman, Bae Hee-bum and three others at his home in Jegi-dong, Dongdaemun-gu, Seoul on December 2, 1947.

They organized the Korean Revolutionary Unit for the purpose of assassinating Chang Duk-soo in August 1947 and they were either officers or vigorous members of the Korean Confederation of Students who supported the Provisional Government.

국제연합(UN)으로 이관시켰네

국제연합 총회 소련 수석 대표 비신스키(Vyshinskii. A. Y.)는
“한국 문제의 국제연합 상정은
 미소 간의 협정을 직접 위반하는 것”
이라고 극구 반대하였지만, 마샬의 제안은
국제연합총회 운영위원회에서 가결되었네(1947. 09. 21.)

미소공동위원회 제62차 본회의(10. 18.)에서
미국 측 수석 대표 브라운 소장이 국제연합에서
한국 문제 토론이 끝날 때까지
공동위원회 업무를 중단하자고 제의했네

소련 측 수석 대표 스티코프는
소련 대표단의 서울 철수를 발표하고
50여 명의 소련 대표단이 평양으로 출발함으로써
제2차 미소공동위원회는 막을 내렸네(1947. 10. 21.)

김구는 이승만의 노선에 협조하는 대신
국민 의회를 중심으로 우익의 단결을 요구하여
이승만의 동의를 얻어냈으나
장덕수의 암살(1947. 12. 02.)로 김구와 이승만
한민당의 단결은 무산되고 말았네

The Korean Confederation of Students was organized in June 2007 and recommended Cho So-ang and Um Hyang-sup as honorary chairmen.

Park Kwang-ok was a current policeman who worked as a sergeant at the Jongro Police Station and Bae Hee-bum was an elementary school teacher and they were the members of the Korean Independence Party.

Kim Gu was suspected to be behind person of the assassination of Chang Duk-soo,
asked for help from Rhee Syng-man.

Rhee Syng-man actually strongly suggested the possible relationship with such an incident saying, "It is unbelievable that President Kim (Kim Gu) would be involved in this incident on purpose".

When Rhee Syng-man tried to form 'Korea National Delegation' in solidarity with the Korea Democratic People's Party staying as looker-on in a crisis due to the assassination of Chang Duk-soo, Kim Gu was angry and absolutely opposed on the sole government and insisted on the dissolution of the 'Korea National Delegation' on December 22, 1947.

서울 동대문구 제기동 자택에서
현직 경찰이던 박광옥朴光玉, 배희범 등 5명이 쏜
총격을 받고 사망한 장덕수(1947. 12. 02.).

장덕수를 암살할 목적으로
대한혁명단을 조직한 이들은(1947. 08.)
임정을 지지하는 대한학생총연맹의 간부 및 맹원들이었네

1947년 6월 결성된 대한학생총연맹은 김구를 총재
조소앙과 엄항섭을 명예위원장으로 추대한 단체였네

박광옥은 종로경찰서의 경사로 근무하는 현역 경찰관이었고
배희범은 초등학교 교사로 모두 한독당 당원이었네

김구는 자신이 장덕수의 암살 배후로 의심받자 「註釋*44」
이승만에게 도움을 요청했네

이승만은
"김주석(김구)이 고의로 이런 일에 관련되었으리라고는
믿을 수 없다."
며 사실상 김구 관련설을 강하게 암시했네

이승만이 한민당과 연대하며

Kim Sung-soo agreed to integrate the Korean Independence Party and the Democratic Party of Korea, meanwhile Chang Duk-soo's view on Kim Gu and Korea Independence Party was changed negative on the occasion of the assassination of Song Jin-wu, and he opposed saying that it was offering the party to the Provisional Government as a whole.

Kim Gu, who had a fierce debate over whether to participate in the US-Soviet Joint Committee, appeared in the court of the US Military Government Court on March 13, 1948 when Kim Suk-hwang and Cho Sang-hang were arrested. They were engaged as officers of the Provisional Government, the Korea Independence Party and the Democratic Representative and were arrested as a result of the assassination of Chang Duk-soo as the behind scene persons.

The dispute continued between Rhee Syng-man who strongly insisted to establish a sole government of South Korea and general Hodge who had not abandoned his lingering affection to form a coalition government in cooperation with Soviet Union. Kim Kyu-sik insisted that the coalition government was the only practicable way to reunite the Korea.

독자적으로 '한국민족대표단' 을 구성하려고 하자
분노한 김구는 단독 정부 절대 반대와
'한국민족대표단' 의 해산을 주장했네(1947. 12. 22.)

한국독립당과 한국민주당의 통합을 김성수는 찬성 하였으나
고하의 암살로 김구와 한독당에 부정적인 장덕수는
당을 통째로 임시 정부에 갖다 바치는 일이라며
한민당과 한독당의 통합에 반대했네

미소공동위원회 참가 여부를 놓고
장덕수와 격렬한 논쟁을 했던 김구는
장덕수의 암살 사건의 배후 인물로
임정과 한독당, 민주 의원에 모두 간부로
몸 담았던 김석황, 조상항이 체포되면서
미 군정청 법정에 출두하였네(1948. 03. 13.)

남한만의 독립 정부 수립을 강력히 주장하는
이승만과 소련과 협조하여 연립 정부를 구성하겠다는
미련을 버리지 못한 하지 장군의 갈등은 계속되었네
김규식은 연립 정부가 한국을 재통일하는 유일하고
실행 가능한 방법이라고 주장하고 있었네

UN Temporary Commission on Korea

After the two times of US-Soviet Joint Committees have broken down, the United States proposed the issue of the Korean peninsula at the United Nations General Assembly in October 1947, the Soviet Union objected that it is violating the decision of the three foreign ministers' meeting in Moscow and it would be the best for the Koreans to solve it by themselves.

The United Nations General Assembly, under the auspices of the Political Commission, adopted "The Resolution No.112 of the North and South Korean General Election" on the 14th of November.

However, in the discussion process that preceded the adoption of the resolution, the devised situation of Korea has not been considered at all.

The Soviet Union said that UN had no authority to deal with this problem because of the previous US?Soviet agreement.

The United Nations composed temporary committee by appointing the representatives of nine countries such as Australia, Canada, China, El

유엔한국임시위원단

두 차례의 미소공동위원회가 결렬된 후
미국이 1947년 10월 유엔 총회에 한반도 문제를 상정하자
소련은 이는 모스크바 3상 회의 결정을 위반하는 것이며
한국 문제는 미 · 소 양군이 철수한 후
조선인 스스로 해결하게 하는 것이
가장 바람직하다면서 반대를 했네

유엔 총회는 정치 위원회 결의를 기초로 유엔 감시하의
'남북총선거안을 결의안 제112호' 를
채택하였네(1947. 11. 14.)「註釋*45」

그러나 결의문 채택에 앞서 행해진 토의 과정에서도
한국의 분단 상황은 전혀 고려되지 않았네
소련은 이전에 이루어진 미소협약 때문에 유엔은
이 문제를 다룰 권한이 없다고 주장했네

오스트레일리아, 캐나다, 중국, 엘살바도르, 프랑스
인도, 필리핀, 시리아, 우크라이나 등

Salvador, France, India, Philippines, Syria, Ukraine, but the Republic of Ukraine denied the commission supporting the statement of the Soviet Union that the UN has no jurisdiction.

According to the UN resolution, the United Nations Commission on the Korean Peninsula (UNC) members arrived in Korea and the first meeting was held on the 12th, and they prepared the general election on January 9, 1948.

Kremara P. S. Menon, the Indian representative, head of the UN temporary committee, asserted that there are also patriotic leaders in North Korea and insisted that "Independence alone is not enough. They must be united." at the rally held at Seoul Sports Stadium where 75,000 people gathered.

Police director Cho Byung-ok, the chief of the welcome committee,urged to achieve "The sacred and urgent mission" as soon as possible.

He replied "As Korea had not yet got a fruit of freedom, political, economic and social challenges are faced the catastrophic crisis."

Provisional delegations requested to both US and Soviet to cooperate with regard to the North and South general election but the Soviet rejected and the delegations were not able to go to North Korea.

9개 국 대표를 위원으로 지명하여
임시위원단을 구성했으나 우크라이나 공화국은
유엔의 관할권이 없다는 소련의 성명을 지지한다며
위원직을 거부했네

유엔의 결의에 따라 입국한 유엔한국임시위원단은 「註釋*46」
12일부터 첫 회의를 갖고 총선거를 준비하였네
(1948. 01. 09.)

유엔임시위원단 단장 인도의 메논(Kremara P. S. Menon)은
7만 5천 명이 운집한 서울운동장의 군중 대회에서
북한에도 애국적 지도자가 있다고 단언하면서
"독립만으로는 부족하다. 단결되어야 한다."
고 주장하자

환영위원회 책임자인 경무국장 조병옥은
"신성하고 긴급한 사명"을 하루 빨리 완수해 달라고 촉구하면서
"한국은 자유의 꽃이 아직 결실을 맺지 못하고 있기 때문에
정치, 경제, 사회적으로 파국의 위기에 직면하고 있다."
고 화답했네

임시위원단은 미, 소 양국에 남북 총선거에 대한 협력을
요청하였으나 소련의 거부로 북한 입북이 좌절되었네

The United Nations Korean Provisional Commission wished to listen to the opinion on the political factors of Korea. Kim Gu and Kim Kyu-sik said that it is impossible to have voluntary election at present, and requested to allow them to go to North Korea even at their risk of death in order for immediate release of the arrested political prisoners, and negotiate with the kidnapped politically important persons.

Kim Kyu-sik and other neutral-right wing powers orientated towards left and right-wing coalition who participated in the US-Soviet Joint Committee were cold on the matter of sole government saying that the South Korean sole government would fix the division of two Koreas, and it will help Military Government's reasonable extension, and the democratic voluntary election can't be guaranteed under the intervention and interruption of foreign powers.

The communists, including the South Korean Labor Party which was judged as illegal, actively objected claiming the People's Committee that insisted Kim Il-sung's "Withdrawal of foreign troops from Korea first and establishment of a unified government thereafter."

Chinese consul Ryu advised to Rhee Syng-man who failed to convince the necessity of election to the delegates of UN Korea Temporary Committee for three days. He advised to Rhee to give impression to the delegates that the division of the Korean leaders was not that much serious not to be solved.

유엔한국임시위원회가
조선의 정치 요인에 관한 의견을 청취키로 하자
김구와 김규식은 현시점에서는 자율 선거가
불가능하다면서 구속된 정치범을 즉시 석방하여
남북 정치 요인의 협상을 위하여
생명을 무릅쓰고라도 북한에 가려 하니
이를 허용해 달라고 요구했네

미소공동위원회에 참여했던
김규식金奎植 중심의 좌우 합작파 중간 우익 세력은
남한만의 단독 선거가 한국의 분단을 고착화하고
군정의 연장을 합리화하며, 외세의 개입과 간섭하에서는
민주적 자율 선거가 보장될 수 없다면서
단독 정부론에 대하여 냉담했네

불법화된 남조선노동당을 비롯한 공산주의자들은
'선 외국군 철수, 후 통일정부 수립' 이라는 김일성金日成의
인민위원회 주장을 내세우며 적극적으로 반대했네

사흘 동안 유엔한국임시위원회 위원들에게
선거의 필요성을 납득시키려 했지만 실패한 이승만에게
중국의 류 영사는 한국의 지도자들의 분열이
해소될 수 없을 정도는 아니라는 인상을

On the 12th of February, the three persons who had a luncheon meeting at the Chinese Consulate agreed to the condition of agreement to have the general election in South Korea.

Rhee Syng-man announced a statement on the 15th of February saying "I did not agree on it from the beginning but if it does not give any obstacle or cause postponement, I will ignore it."

Australia, Canada, India and Syria sought ways to reunify Korea and China, Philippines, El Salvador supported the establishment of South Korean sole government saying that persuasion of Soviet was not possible.

On the 28th of February, there was a heated debate on the agendas to approve an independent election in sole South Korea and another agenda to support the limited purpose of "regional" election electing national representatives who will be the negotiators in South Korea at the Provisional UN General Assembly.

The United States insisted on joining North Korea after the establishment of a realistic central government in South Korea as two-thirds of the total population is in South Korea.

위원들에게 주어야 한다는 조언을 했네

12월 12일, 중국 영사관에서 오찬 회담을 가진
이승만, 김구, 김규식은 남한의 총선거 실시에 동의한다는
조건에 합의했네(이승만의 대미투쟁 上 229~233p)

이어서 김구와 김규식이 제안한 남북 요인 회담에 대해 「註釋*47」

"나는 처음부터 찬성하지 않았으나 이 문제가 총선거에
대하여 지장을 초래하거나 시일이 연기되는
폐단이 없다면 방임하겠다."
는 이승만의 담화가 발표되었네(이승만의 대미투쟁 上 231p)

오스트레일리아, 캐나다, 인도, 시리아는
한국이 재통일될 수 있는 방안을 모색했고,
중국, 필리핀, 엘살바도르는 소련의 설득이
불가능하다며 남한만의 정부 수립을 지지했네

2월 28일, 유엔 임시총회는 남한 단독 선거를 승인 안건과
남한에서 협의 대상자가 될 국민 대표자를 선출한다는
제한된 목적의 '지역' 선거를 지원하는 안건에 대한
격렬한 토의가 벌어졌네

China and the Philippines expressed their opinion to establish a government in South Korea immediately.

Argentina insisted that "We should not say in the way that we allow independence to Korea,Independence is the right of Koreans and it should be declared in the way they wish".

Canada insisted that the election only in South Korea is illegal saying that the election must be held throughout whole Korean peninsula according to the resolution of November 14, 1947 claiming that it is not wise to formalize the division of the peninsula.

Australia was against the split election only in South Korea because there would be two hostile governments on the Korean Peninsula.

At the end of the heated debate, they decided to execute the election "In the area of the peninsula where the Commission is accessible", according to the result of votes of 31 agree, 2 oppose, and 11 abstain.

미국은 남한에 전체 인구의 2/3가 있기 때문에
남한에 정부를 수립하고 북한을 합류시켜야 한다고 주장했네

중국, 필리핀은
남한에 정부를 즉각 수립해야 한다는 의견을 표명했네

"우리는 마치 한국에 독립을 허용해 준다는 식으로
말해서는 안 된다. 독립은 한국인의 권리이며
그들이 원하는 방식으로 천명되어야 한다."
고 아르헨티나는 주장했네

캐나다는 1947년 11월 14일 결의안에 따라 한반도 전역에
선거를 실시해야 한다며 남한만의 단독 선거는 불법적이며
한반도의 분단을 공식화하는 현명치 못한 일이라고 주장했네

오스트레일리아는
한반도에 두 개의 적대적인 정부가 생기는 것이기 때문에
남한만의 분리 선거는 반대한다는 주장을 폈네

격렬한 토의 끝에 유엔 임시총회는
찬성 31, 반대 2, 기권 11의 투표 결과에 따라
"위원단이 접근 가능한 한반도의 지역에서"
선거를 실시한다고 결정했네

Canada and Australia were opposed and the communists abstained to emphasize their already established position that the UN's jurisdiction over the Korean issue is illegal.

The sole election of South Korea was finalized but various obstacles were scattered here and there.

The important thing was the disagreement among the three people, Rhee Syng-man, Kim Gu, and Kim Kyu-sik.

All the three persons were self-centered and they believed that they were real patriots, and only they had the leadership that is required for the establishment of the country.

General Hodge of the US Military Government was supporting Kim Kyu-sik to be the presidential candidate for the new government.

When the general election of South Korea was decided, Kim Gu declared that he would continue his struggle in order for the realization of the unification of the fatherland and for the complete independent by hoisting the flag of justice and together with a majority of patriotic people saying that the Peoples' Republic of North Korea also opposes it.

Kim Kyu-sik said that he will not participate in the election even if the two Koreas hold unified general elections after the transitional period. He will not oppose South Korean election and declared that he will not participate

캐나다와 오스트레일리아는 반대하였고
공산권은 한국 문제에 대한 유엔의 관할은 불법이라는
기존 입장을 강조하기 위해 기권을 했네

남한만의 단독 선거가 확정되었으나
여러 가지 걸림돌이 곳곳에 산적해 있었네

중요한 것은 이승만, 김구, 김규식 3인의 의견 불일치였네

세 사람 모두 자기 중심적이며 진정한 애국자들 이였으며
자신만이 건국에 필요한 리더십을 갖고 있다고 믿고 있었네

미 군정의 하지 장군은
김규식을 새 정부의 대통령 후보로 밀고 있었네

김구는 남한만의 단독 선거는
북한의 인민공화국도 반대하고 있다며
정의의 깃발을 잡고 절대 다수의 애국 동포들과 함께
조국의 통일과 완전 자주 독립을 실현하기 위하여
계속 분투하겠다고 선언했네

김규식은 나는 과도입의過渡立議일만 끝나면
남북이 통일된 총선거라 할지라도 참가하지 않겠다

in the political action. (February 28, 1948. Kyunghyang Daily Newspaper)

From the end of 1947, the Soviet Union called North Korea as "Democratic People's Republic of Korea".

The legal experts dispatched from Moscow to North Korea drafted the North Korean Constitution based on the constitution that was created for the Eastern European Satellite countries and reported it to the Soviet Ministry of Foreign Affairs and the Soviet Communist Party.

The Central Committee of the Soviet Communist Party studied it in detail and ordered to the Soviet Military Government in Pyongyang to reflect it as it is on the Constitution of the Democratic People's Republic of Korea.

The Central Committee of the Soviet Communist Party ordered as follows:

"Do not deliberate the draft constitution at this meeting and open it to the people and let it be discussed by whole people in order to reflect the North Korean people's needs. And convene the meeting of North Korean people in March 1948 to approve the draft of the Constitution.

남조선 선거는 반대하지 않으며 앞으로 정치 행동은
불참하겠다고 천명했네(1948. 2. 28. 경향신문)

소련 군정은 1947년 말부터 북한의 국호를
'조선민주주의인민공화국' 이라 정했네

모스크바로부터 파견된 법률 전문가들은
동유럽 위성국을 창설할 때
작성한 헌법을 참고하여 작성한 북조선 헌법초안을
소련 외무성과 소련공산당에 보고했네

소련공산당 중앙위원회는 세부적으로 검토를 마친 후
조선민주주의인민공화국 헌법에 그대로 반영할 것을
평양의 소련 군정에 지령했네 「註釋*48」

소련공산당 중앙위원회는 이 지령에서

"헌법 초안은 이 회의에서 심의하지 말고 헌법위원회가
작성한 헌법 초안에 대한 조선 인민의 요구를 충분히
반영할 수 있도록 초안을 공개해서 전 인민의 토의에 붙이고
임시 헌법 초안 검토 승인을 위한
북조선인민회의를 1948년 3월 소집하라."
고 명령했네

Kim Gu and Kim Kyu-sik expressed political views to both North and South leaders in the UN Interim Commission on the Korean Peninsula "To have North and South general election having the discussion between the North and South political leaders after the simultaneous withdrawal of US and Soviet army in North and South.

They proposed to have political leaders meeting to have North and South general election and to establish the unified government to both Kim Il-sung and Kim Du-bong in written on the 16th of February.

Kim Il-sung immediately made a correction of proposal to open the meeting in the form of joint conference of representatives of the whole Korean political parties and social groups.

On February 7, 1948, the People's Assembly released the draft of the Korean Constitution that was prepared by the Constitution Committee for the people's discussion.

In March, they decided to convene the People's Assembly to approve the draft constitution.But due to certain reason, they reported to A. Bisinski, the Soviet Communist Party Central Committee International Secretary (former ambassador to the United Nations) that the convening of the People's Assembly will be postponed to April.

유엔한국임시위원회에서 남북 지도자에게
"미, 소 양 지구 주둔군의 동시 철수한 후
 남북 정치 지도자가 협의하여 남북 총선거 실시하자."
는 정치적 견해를 밝힌 김구와 김규식은

남북한 총선거와 통일 정부 수립을 위한
남북한 정치지도자회의를
김일성과 김두봉金枓奉에게 서신으로 제의했네(1948. 02. 16.)

이에 김일성은
전조선정당사회단체대표자 연석회의의 형태로
남북한 정치지도자 회의를 열자고 수정 제의를 했네

1948년 2월 7일, 인민회의는 인민회의 헌법위원회에서 준비한
조선 헌법 초안을 전 인민의 토의에 붙이기 위해 공개했네

인민회의는 오는 3월에 헌법 초안 승인을 위해
인민회의를 소집하기로 결정했으나
사정상 인민회의 소집을 4월로 연기한다는 내용을
소련공산당 중앙 위원회 국제 담당 비서
비신스키(A. Bisinski 유엔 주재 소련 대사 역임)에게
보고를 했네 「**註釋*49**」

On the 6th April, major general Lebedev (political commander) received an order from general Stykov (Stalin's plenipotentiary to North Korea, the military commissioner of the Soviet army in Yeonhae military district) as follows:

"Carry out the four guidelines for the Sovietization of the Korean Peninsula by declaring to open the North and South Korean political representatives' joint meeting that Kim Gu and Kim Kyu-sik proposed. Call Kim Gu and Kim Kyu-sik to Pyongyang to oppose the South Korea's sole general election. Expel the UN Korean Provisional Commission, and make the Soviet and US forces withdraw simultaneously from the Korean peninsula. Hold the North and South Korean general election to establish a provisional government after withdrawing foreign troops from the Korean peninsula."

Kim Il-sung and Kim Du-bong proposed to major general Lebedev (political commander) on the 8th of April as follows:

"We adopt the constitution at this meeting, but for the time being, we will not organize the cabinet. We will give position to Kim Gu and Kim Kyu-sik and will persuade them proposing to establish the unified government after the constitution is passed."

4월 6일, 레베데프 소장(정치 사령관)은

"김구와 김규식이 제의한 남북한정치대표자연석회의를
 평양에서 열겠다고 발표한 후
 김구와 김규식을 평양으로 불러들인다.
 연석회의 의결로 남조선만의 총선을 반대하고
 조선에서 유엔한국임시위원회 추방한다.
 임시 정부를 수립하기 위한 남북 총선거는
 소련군과 미군이 철수 후 실시한다는 등
 한반도의 소비에트화를 위한 네 가지 지침을 관철하라."
는 지령을 「註釋*50」 스티코프 대장(소련군 연해군구
군사위원, 스탈린의 북한 문제 전권 대사)으로부터 받았네

김일성과 김두봉은 레베데프 소장(정치 사령관)에게

"이번 회의에서 헌법은 채택하지만
 당분간 내각은 구성하지 않고
 김구와 김규식에게 직위를 부여하여
 헌법이 통과된 후 통일 정부를 세울 것이라고 제의하여
 두 사람을 회유할 계획이다."
는 의견을 제시했네(1948. 04. 08.) 「註釋*51」

소련 군정은 김구와 김규식이

The Soviet Union Military Government had a record that if Kim Gu and Kim Kyu-sik break or leave the joint conference, they will be taken as the "US spy" and in addition, according to a report on the situation received from South Korea, Kim Gu would say to the reporters "I know that there is a scheme to assassinate me by the 10th of May" on the 17th of April.

Kim Gu asked to Kim Il-sung at his sole meeting with Kim Il-sung on the 3rd of May

"If the US Military Government strongly presses me, shall I expect that North Korea would give me a shelter?" The record says that Kim Il-sung answered positively.

Kim Gu had a meeting with reporters who are in charge of Gyunggyojang Office before going to North Korea and said resolutely:

"I don't have great expectations that the inter-Korean talks would be successful.

But I would only like to appeal them. Even one case in ten thousand, I can't come back home from the North, please deliver this message to our three million compatriots that I fought to the end for our country's independence"

전조선정당사회단체대표자연석회의를
결렬시키거나 퇴장하면
이들을 '미제 간첩' 으로 몰아간다는 대책과 함께
남한으로부터 받은 정세 보고서에서 김구가 기자들에게
"나를 5월 10일까지 암살하려는 것을 알고 있다."
고 기록하고 있네(1948. 04. 17.). 「註釋*52」

김일성과의 단독 회담(1948. 05. 03.)에서 김구는
"만일 미 군정이 나를 강하게 압박하면 북한이 나에게
피난처를 제공해 줄 것이라는 기대를 할 수 있는가?"
질문했네

그 질문에
김일성은 "긍정적으로 대답했다."
고 비망록에서 기록하고 있네 「註釋*53」

김구는 북행을 앞두고 경교장 출입 기자단과의 간담회에서

"남북 회담이 성공되라는 큰 기대를 갖고 있는 것은 아니다.
단지 통사정이라도 해 보려 한다.
자신이 이번 북행에서 만에 하나 돌아오지 못하더라도
내가 독립을 위해서 끝까지 싸웠다는 것을
삼천만 동포에게 전해 주기 바란다."

Kim Gu, Kim Kyu-sik, Cho So-ang, Cho Wan-gu participated in the meeting of representatives of the whole Korean political parties and social organizations held on the 22nd of April with expectation of establishing an unified independent government through peaceful negotiations with North Korean communists in accordance with the principles of national self-determination.

The agenda of the Representatives Meeting was already adopted "To oppose the resolution of UN and sole election of South Korea and its sole government."

Kim Il-sung promoted abroad in the meeting during April 19-28, 1948 that the Constitution of the Democratic People's Republic of Korea that was adopted in the joint meeting of the whole Korean political parties and social organizations is the only constitution that reflects the will of the whole Korean people.

Kim Gu went to the Magog temple in Gongju, Chungnam-do announcing a brief statement after attending at the summit meeting of the whole Korean political parties and social group representatives which was convened in order for the Communists to oppose the general election in South Korea.

The following Kim Kyu-sik's statement was a statement confirming that the inter-Korean negotiations were humiliating negotiation.

는 비장한 발언을 하였네「註釋*54」

김구, 김규식, 조소앙趙素昻, 조완구趙琬九 등은
민족 자결주의 원칙에 따라
북한 공산주의자들과의 평화적 협상을 통한
독립된 통일 정부 수립을 기대하고 평양에서 개최된
전조선 정당사회단체 대표자 연석회의에
참석했네(1948. 04. 22.)「註釋*55」

"유엔의 결정과 남조선 단독 선거 및 단독정부를 반대한다."
는 대표자 연석회의 의제는 이미 채택되어 있었네

북남대표가 합의한 전조선정당사회단체 대표자 연석회의에서
채택된 조선민주주의인민공화국 헌법은「註釋*56」
전 조선 인민의 의사가 반영된 단 하나의 헌법이라고
김일성은 대외적으로 선전했네(1948. 04. 19.~28. 개최)

김일성이 남한의 총선거를 반대하기 위하여 소집한
전조선 정당사회단체 대표자 연석회의에 참석하고 돌아온
김구는 간단한 성명을 발표한 뒤 공주의 마곡사로 내려갔네

"이제는 단독 정부를 반대하지 않는다.
물론 나는 남북 협상에 책임을 지고

“I do not oppose the sole government from now on. Of course, I take the responsibility for inter-Korean negotiations and I will not participate in the elections.”

The political forces supporting Rhee Syng-man’s establishing sole government said that the general election in South Korea is a realistic step toward establishing a unified government.
Korea Democratic Party, Chosun Democratic Party and Korean Independence Promotion People’s Conference insisted that the solution of Korean problem can be solved fundamentally by cultivating democratic capabilities of the people.

The general election date was decided by Menon K. P. S., the chairman of the Korean Temporary Committee ‘The period will not to be delayed in the first week of May 1948’ and at the request of lieutenant general J. R. Hodge, the head of the US Military Government, it was decided as the 9th of May, but it was changed definitely to the 10th of May because the 9th of May was Sunday.

It was a free election that accepted the four principles of common, equal, secret, and direct election.

The electoral system has adopted a small electoral district system to elect one person from one district.

The United Nations Temporary Commission on Korean Affairs held a

선거에도 참여하지 않겠다."
는 김규식의 성명은 남북 협상이
굴욕적인 협상이었음을 자인한 성명이었네

이승만의 단독 정부 수립을 지지하는 정치 세력은
남한의 총선거는 통일 정부 수립으로 가는 현실적인 단계이며
한국 문제 해결은 근본적으로 국민들 사이에
민주주의 역량을 배양함으로써 해결할 수 있다고 주장한
한국민주당, 조선민주당과 대한독립촉성국민회 등이었네

총선거일은 한국임시위원단 메논(Menon, K. P. S.) 의장이
정한 '1948년 5월 제1주에서 지연되지 않는 기간' 을
미 군정의 하지(J. R. Hodge) 중장의 요청에 따라 5월 9일로
결정되었으나 5월 9일이 일요일이라는 이유로
5월 10일로 변경 확정되었네

보통, 평등, 비밀, 직접의 4대 원칙을 수용한 자유 선거였네

선거구제는 1선거구에서 1인을 선출하는
소선거구제를 채택했네

유엔한국임시위원단은 남북한을 통하여 인구 비례에 따라
선출될 총 300석의 국회의원 의석 중

general election only in South Korea that will elect 200 seats legislators out of total 300 seats deducting 100 seats in North Korea where election is not available.

All men and women over 21 years of age were entitled to vote in the election.
The qualification for election was granted to all citizens over 25 years of age except;
Those who got title of nobility by the Japanese government,
Those who were the members of the Japanese Imperial Assembly,
Those who were judges and commissioned officers or higher at time of Japanese rule,
Those who were Police officers, MPs, MP assistants, those with a grade of 3 high officials or higher,
Those who were in the position of higher police officers and those who received more than 7 credits of medal,
Moon Cham-eui, the deputy chairman of the Jungchuwon Society, the advisory organization to the Japanese governor's office, were deprived of his right to be elected.

As the election law of the National Assembly was promulgated on the 17th of March, during 20 days from 20th of March to 9th of April, the total number of voters was 8,132,517 and 7,840,871 people or 96.4% of them were listed on the electoral roll and 95.5% of the enrollees participated in the voting.

선거가 불가능한 북한 지역 의석수 100석을 제외한
200석의 국회의원을 선출하는 남한만의 총선거를 실시했네

만 21세 이상의 모든 남녀 국민에게 선거권이 부여되었네

피선거권은 만 25세 이상의 모든 국민에게 인정되었으나
일본 정부로부터 작위를 받은 자나
일본제국의회의 의원이었던 자와
일제 때에 판관, 임관 이상인 자
경찰관, 헌병, 헌병보, 고등관 3등급 이상인 자
고등 경찰의 직에 있던 자 및 훈勳 7등 이상을 받은 자
중추원의 부의장, 문참의 등은 피선거권이 박탈되었네

미 군정법령으로 국회의원 선거법이 공포(1948. 03. 17.)되자
3월 20일부터 4월 9일까지 20일 간 총유권자 813만 2,517인 중
96.4%에 해당하는 784만 871인이 선거인 명부에 등재되어
선거인 명부 등록자 95.5%가 투표에 참여했네

총선에는 모두 948인이 입후보하여
평균 4.7 : 1의 경쟁률을 보였으며
대한독립촉성국민회가 235인의 후보자를 내어 가장 많았고
48개 정당, 사회 단체에서 후보를 냈네

There were 948 candidates in the general election with an average of 4.7: 1.

The Korea Independence Promotion People's Conference had the largest number of 235 candidates and 48 political parties and social organizations showed candidates.

As a result of the election, Parliamentarians were elected as follows;

85 non-partisans, 55 Korea Independence Promotion People's Conference members, 28 Korea Democratic Party, 12 Daedong Youth Party, 6 Chosun National Youth Party, 2 Korea Independence Farmers Promotion Federation and 12 others.

Ji Chung-chun in Sungdong-gu, Seoul got the highest number of winning votes in the election with 41,582 votes, and Cho Joong-hyun of Jangdan-gun, Gyeonggi-do, got the lowest number of votes with 2,792 votes. The automatically elected persons with no voting were 12, or 6% of the total number of the members.

The elected constitutional assemblymen composed 'Preparatory Committee for Assembly' with Shin Ik-hee as its chairman on the 21st of May after having negotiations with US Military Government.

On the 27th of May, a total of 143 members of the National Assembly assumed the regulations on the operation of the National Assembly including the procedures of opening ceremony to the Preparatory Committee until the National Assembly Act is enacted, and set the date of opening of the Constitutional Assembly to the 31st of May.

선거 결과 선출된 국회의원은
무소속 85인, 대한독립촉성국민회 55인, 한국민주당 28인
대동청년당 12인, 조선민족청년당 6인
대한독립촉성농민총연맹 2인 기타 12명이었네

당선자 중 최고득표자는
서울 성동구의 지청천으로 4만 1,582표를 얻었네
최저 득표자는
경기도 장단군의 조중현趙重顯으로 총 2,792표이었네
무투표 당선자는 의원 정수의 6%에 해당하는 12인이었네

제헌 국회 당선자들은 미 군정과 협의를 가진 끝에
5월 21일, 신익희 의원을 위원장으로 하는
'국회 소집을 위한 준비 위원회'를 구성했네

5월 27일, 국회의원 당선자 143명이 참석한
'국회의원예비회의'에서
국회법이 제정될 때까지
개원식 절차 등을 포함한 국회 운영에 관한 규정을
준비위원회에 위임하고
제헌 국회 개원 일자를 5월 31일로 정했네

5월 31일 오전 10시 20분, 감격적인 제헌 국회가 개원했네

On the 31st of May 10:20 am, finally an emotional Constitutional Assembly was opened.

The eldest Rhee Syng-man was recommended as temporary chairman and prayed prior to opening speech as follows;

"First of all, we should thank God to open here the first session of the Democratic Independent Korea. Whatever the religion, ideology the Korean people may have, we may not be able to boast of only the power of our people facing today's situation.
Therefore, we can't but give thanks to God.
I suggest that we all stand up to thank God with faithfulness.
Legislator Lee Yoon-young, please lead the pray to God briefly."

As soon as all the legislators stood up,
Lee Yoon-young went up to the stand and started to pray;

"God, you created the universe and all things in the world.
And you are taking care of human history with Providence.
We thank to our Lord with sincerity for taking care of our nation
And your blessing our land with full of thanks to have today.

For a long time
Our God heard the suffering and appeal of this nation
Took the sword of justice

최연장자인 이승만을 임시 의장에 추대했네
임시 의장 이승만은 개회사에 앞서

"대한민국 독립 민주국 제1차 회의를 여기서 열게 된 것을
 우리가 먼저 하나님께 감사해야 할 것입니다.
 종교, 사상 무엇을 가지고 있든지(대한민국 국민은)
 누구나 오늘을 당해 가지고 사람의 힘으로만 된 것이라고
 우리는 자랑할 수 없을 것입니다.
 그러므로 하나님께 감사를 드리지 않을 수 없습니다.
 나는 먼저 우리가 다 성심으로 일어서서
 하나님에게 감사를 드리고자 합니다.
 이윤영 의원 나오셔서 간단한 말씀으로
 하나님에게 기도를 올려 주시기를 바랍니다."

국회의원 모두가 일어서자
단상에 오른 이윤영 의원의 기도가 시작되었네

"우주와 만물을 창조하시고
 인간의 역사를 섭리하시는 하나님이시여
 이 민족을 돌아보시고 이 땅을 축복하셔서
 감사에 넘치는 오늘이 있게 해 주신 주님께
 저희들은 성심으로 감사하나이다.
 오랜 시일 동안

Curved the Japanese violence
Now you moved the conscience of the whole world
You listened to the wish of our people
We believe that Your providence showed up globally
And You made this joyful and historical time
To come to us

O, God!
From now on,
Please redress a grievance of
Our nation's suffering hardships and shame
Of being divided into two parts of North and South.
We pray that the day would come shortly
When our nation, our compatriots would
Sing songs hand in hand laughing altogether.

O, God!
The longer the suffering of citizens that no one ever wanted
The power of the devil will be expanded more onto the earth,
We consider that the holy glory of our God
Necessarily come to this land.
We pray You would allow Korea to be independent and unified. .
In addition, please allow us happiness of the citizens
And allow us the global peace as well.

이 민족의 고통과 호소를 들으시고
정의의 칼을 빼서
일제의 폭력을 굽히신 하나님께서
이제 세계 만방의 양심을 움직이시고
또한 우리 민족의 염원을 들으심으로
이 기쁜 역사적 환희의 날을
이 시간 우리에게 오게 하심은
하나님의 섭리가 세계 만방에
성시하신 것으로 저희들은 믿나이다.

하나님이시여!
이로부터 남, 북이 둘로 갈리어진
이 민족의 어려운 고통과 수치를
신원伸冤하여 주시고
우리 민족 우리 동포가 손을 같이 잡고 웃으며
노래 부르는 날이 우리 앞에 속히 오기를
기도하나이다.

하나님이시여!
원치 아니한 민생의 도탄은 길면 길수록
이 땅에 악마의 권세가 확대되나
하나님의 거룩하신 영광은
이 땅에 오지 않을 수밖에 없을 줄

Relying on the holy will of God,
We have been chosen holy to become literally representatives of the nation.
However, we feel that our responsibility is so important
But we are so powerless and we pray to You
To provide us the elements such as knowledge, patience and courage
As You are the fountain of all the virtues.

Now that the Assembly is established,
Our desire is that all of our problems
That our nation is eagerly wishing to be solved smoothly and
The world is paying attention and waiting.
And may the day of complete independence come to this land
And let us accomplish this task that we set up
That will be bright and green future history generation to generation.

저희들은 생각하나이다.
원컨대 우리 조선 독립과 함께
남북 통일을 주시옵고
또한 우리 민생의 복락과 아울러
세계 평화를 허락하여 주시옵소서.

거룩하신 하나님의 뜻에 의지하여
저희들은 성스럽게 택함을 입어 가지고
글자 그대로 민족의 대표가 되었습니다.
그러하오나 우리들의 책임이 중차대한 것을
저희들은 느끼고 우리 자신이
진실로 무력한 것을 생각할 때
지智와 인仁과 용勇과 모든 덕의 근원이 되시는
하나님 앞에 이러한 요소를
저희들이 간구하나이다.

이제 이로부터 국회가 성립이 되어서
우리 민족의 염원이 되는
모든 세계 만방이 주시하고 기다리는
우리의 모든 문제가 원만히 해결되며
또한 이로부터 우리의 완전 자주 독립이
이 땅에 오며, 자손 만대에 빛나고 푸르른 역사를
저희들이 정하는 이 사업을 완수하게 하여 주시옵소서

O, God!
May God give health to the chairman who presides this meeting,
And may God allow health to all the attending representatives,
Please help them to accomplish this task by winning with the justice of conscience
And pride.

We glorify the name of our God and appreciate to God
For today's excitement and
National joy of our historical first step
We pray in the name of our Jesus Christ with thanks.
Amen.

하나님
이 회의를 사회하시는 의장으로부터
모든 의원 일동에게 건강을 주시옵고
또한 이겨서 양심의 정의와 위신을 가지고
이 업무를 완수하게 도와 주시옵기를
기도하나이다.

역사의 첫걸음을 걷는
오늘의 환희와 감격에 넘치는
이 민족적 기쁨을
다 하나님께 영광과 감사를 올리나이다.
이 모든 말씀을 주 예수 그리스도 이름 받들어
기도하나이다. 아멘"

Epilogue

Liberation itself was not the independence.
The liberated space with no independence
Become the outpost of the cold war.

The unrefined freedom gave pains each other
They were sick altogether.
Liberation with no independence was serious pains.

Those who have been tamed by the rule of kings for four thousand years
Shouted the restoration of the national sovereignty
Experiencing the 36 years of Japanese colonial rule,
The pursuit of nationality was different depending on persons.

They have never experienced the politics
Of which the owner is the people
Only was able to raise their voices at their own will.

Totalitarianism pursuing people's democracy

Socialism in pursuit of social democracy
Capitalism in pursuit of liberal democracy

에필로그

해방解放이 곧 독립은 아니었네
독립獨立되지 못한 해방 공간은
냉전冷戰의 전초 기지가 됐네

정제精製되지 않은 자유가
서로를 아프게 했네. 서로가 아팠네
독립 없는 해방은 시리도록 아팠네

4천 년 동안 왕권 통치에 길들여졌던 사람들
36년 동안 일제 식민지 치하治下를 거치면서
국권 회복國權回復을 외쳤지만

추구하는 국체國體는 저마다 달랐네

국민國民이 주인主人인 정치政治를
한 번도 체득體得해 보지 못했기에
소견所見대로 목청을 높였던 사람들

인민 민주주의를 추구하는 전체주의

Regardless of our will
Our national fate had to cross the heaven and the hell
For the past three years.

The pioneers who shouted independence
Moving Manchuria, Chinese continent and Eurasia
Caused by the sorrow of losing nation
Sang songs crying so bitterly;
"Until that day when the East Sea's waters run dry and Mt. Baekdu is worn away,

May God preserve our country for ten thousand years!
Hibiscus and three thousand-li full of splendid rivers and mountains; [*)]
Great Korean people, to the great Korean way, stay always true!"

In the chaos of gap among the super powers
We could get the independence, although we were not able to be
self-reliant the country was born finally where the people are the owners.

It was the grace of God, the work of God.
"A bruised reed He will not break,
And a smoldering wick He will not snuff out"

[*)] 4km is 10 'li' in Korea.

사회 민주주의를 추구하는 사회주의
자유 민주주의를 추구하는 자본주의

우리의 의지와는 상관없이
우리의 운명은 지난 3년 동안
천국과 지옥을 넘나들고 있었네

나라 잃은 설움에 만주 벌판을
중국 대륙과 유라시아를 떠돌며
독립을 외쳤던 선구자들이 목 놓아 불렀던

"동해물과 백두산이 마르고 닳도록
 하나님이 보우하사 우리나라 만세
 무궁화 삼천 리 화려강산
 대한 사람 대한으로 길이 보전하세."

열강의 틈바구니에 낀 혼돈混沌 속에서
독립獨立은 되었으나 자립自立은 아직 할 수 없는
국민이 주인 된 나라가 드디어 탄생했네

상한 갈대 꺾지 않고
꺼져 가는 등불 끄지 않는
하나님의 은혜였네, 하나님의 역사였네

註釋*1 – 스탈린의 대숙청

스탈린(Iosif Vissarionovich Stalin)이 1937년 10월 극동 지방에 거주하는 한인(韓人)의 대부분인 17만 1,781명을 중앙 아시아의 황무지로 강제 이주시켜 2만 명 이상의 목숨을 앗은 것도 대숙청의 일부다.

註釋*2 – 88정찰여단

구소련 국방부 극비 문서인 구소련 극동군 제88 특별저격 경찰 여단 파일 입수로, 그 동안 논란이 있었던 북한의 김일성이 1942년 6월부터 1945년 9월까지 3년 3개월 동안 구소련군 대위로 복무했던 이 여단의 정체 등이 50년 만에 적나라하게 드러났다. – 중앙일보(1992.06.15.) 기사 – 모스크바 = 김국후 특파원

註釋*3 – 조선의 신탁통치

루즈벨트(Franklin Delano Roosevelt) 대통령은 1943년 3월에 이르러 신탁 통치안을 미국의 정책으로 채택하였으며, 이 결정은 다음날, 〈시카고 썬(Chicago Sun)〉지에 보도되었는데 이승만(李承晩)이 격분했음은 물론이다. 그는 15일 미국 대통령에게 신랄한 어조의 항의문을 보냈다. "한국 사람들은 독립을 원하는 것이지 신탁 통치를 원하는 것이 아니다. 미국은 1905년 한국 병탄을 허락함으로써 한국 사람들이 36년 동안이나 고초를 겪어야 했는데, 만일 미국 정치가들이 한국에 독립을 허용하지 않는다면, 미국 자체가 장차 더 큰 환난을 당하게 될 것"이라고 했다. – 이정식의 《이승만 연구》 p414~415.

註釋*4 – 카이로 선언문 중에서

미국의 루즈벨트 대통령은 카이로 선언에서 "현재 조선인이 노예 상태에 놓여 있음에 유의해 앞으로 적절한 절차에 따라 조선인에게 자유와 독립을 줄 것을 합의했다.

註釋*5 – 적절한 절차에 따라

1943년 11월 23일 오후 8시 카이로 회담에는 루즈벨트와 처칠, 장제스가 참석했고 루즈벨트 보좌관 합킨스와 장제스의 통역으로 부인 숭메이링(宋美齡)과 왕충후이(王忠輝) 비서실장이 동석했다. 미국과 중국이 조선, 인도차이나 및 타이(Thailand)의 장래에 대한 상호 이해에 도달하자는 루즈벨트의 제안에 장제스 총통은 "조선에 독립을 부여하는 것이 좋겠다."고 말했고, 루즈벨트는 동의했으나 처칠은 부정적이었다.

11월 24일 루즈벨트는 합킨스에게 합의서 초안을 작성하게 했다. 한국에 관한 사항은 "한국민의 노예 상태에 유의하여 '가능한 한 가장 이른 시기에(at the earlist possible moment)' 한국을 자유롭게 독립시킬 것을 결의한다."였다. 초안을 검토한 루즈벨트는 자신의 신탁 통치 구상을 고려하여 '가능한 한 가장 이른 시기에' 라는 문구를 '적절한 순간에(at the proper moment)' 로 수정했다.

11월 23일 하오 3시 30분, 미국 초안과 영국 초안을 놓고 열린 최종 조율 회의에서 영국 측은 "조선이 자유롭게 독립된다."를 "조선이 일본 통치에서 해방된다."로 수정하자고 제의했다. 수정안이 받아들여지지 않는다면, 조선 문제에 대해 영국 내각은 다룬 적이 없고,

소련의 태도도 알 수가 없기 때문에 조선의 독립에 관한 조항은 성명 문안에서 삭제하자고 주장했다. 중국은 영국의 주장이 '난센스'라며 강력히 반발, 조선이 일본 침략의 첫 번째 희생양이었음을 상기시켰다.

루즈벨트가 카이로 회담에 동석한 해리만 소련 주재 미국 대사에게 의견을 물었다. 해리만은 "소련의 태도에 신경을 쓸 필요가 없다."고 밝혔다. 조선 독립의 의제는 미국과 중국의 강력한 지원으로 살아남았다. 루즈벨트가 수정한 '적절한 순간에' 라는 문구가 카이로 선언의 최종안에서 "적절한 절차를 거쳐서(in due couse)"로 바뀌게 된 것은 영국의 의견이 반영된 것이다. "적절한 절차를 거쳐서"는 처칠 수상이 즐겨 사용하는 단골 문구였다.

註釋*6 – 얄타 회담(Yalta Conference)

점령 방법을 논의하기 위해 크림 반도 얄타에서 회담을 가졌다. 극동 문제에 있어서는 비밀의정서를 채택하였는데, 그것은 소련이 독일 항복 후 2～3개월 이내에 대일전(對日戰)에 참전해야 하며, 그 대가로 연합국은 소련에게 러일전쟁에서 잃은 영토를 반환해 준다는 것이었다.

註釋*7 – 포츠담 협정(Potsdam Agreement)

1945년 영국, 미국, 소련 3개 국 수뇌 사이에 열린 포츠담회담에서 조인된 독일의 전후 처리 방침에 관한 협정이다.

註釋*8 – 조선건국준비위원회(朝鮮建國準備委員會)

1945년 8 · 15 광복 후 여운형(呂運亨)이 중심이 되어 조직한 최초의 건국 준비 단체로, 약칭하여 '건준(建準)' 이라고도 한다. 1945년 8월 초 일본의 패배가 확실해지자 조선 총독 아베 노부유키〔阿部信行〕는 한국에 있는 일본인들의 생명과 재산을 보호해 줄 협상 대상자로 한국의 민족 지도자를 찾았다.

이때 건국 준비를 위한 민족의 대표기관과 정치 세력 형성의 필요성을 느끼고 있던 여운형이 그에 동조함으로써 협상이 이루어지게 되었다. 이에 따라 1944년 8월 10일 비밀리에 '건국 동맹' 이 조직되었고 1945년 8월 15일 광복절 날 조선건국준비위원회를 발족하였다.

註釋*9 – 몽양 여운형의 11차례 테러

1945년 8월 18일 –1차 테러, 1945년 9월 07일 –2차 테러, 1945년 12월 상순 –3차 테러, 1946년 01월 –4차 테러, 1946년 04월 18일 –5차 테러, 1946년 05월 하순 –6차 테러, 1946년 07월 17일 –7차 테러, 1946년 10월 07일 –8차 테러, 1947년 03월 17일 –9차 테러, 1947년 05월 12일 저녁 7시경 –10차 테러, 1947년 07월 19일 오후 1시경 – 11차 테러.

註釋*10 – 조선인민공화국(朝鮮人民共和國)

8 · 15 광복 직후 발족한 여운형(呂運亨) 중심의 조선 건국 준비 위원회가 정치적 주도권을 장악하기 위해 선포한 나라 이름.

註釋*11 - 미 군정(美軍政)

1945년 일본의 항복으로 삼팔선(한반도 북위 38° 선) 이남 지역에 미군이 진주하여 9월 8일부터 1948년 8월 15일 남한 단독 정부가 수립되기까지 3년 동안 실시한 미군의 통치 시기.

註釋*12 - 소련의 군정 통치

1945년 8월 9일 종전을 며칠 앞두고 대일 선전 포고를 한 소련군은 다음날인 10일부터 북한으로 진주했다. 당시는 이미 일본의 패전이 완연하던 때여서 소련군은 거의 아무런 저항도 받지 않고 북한을 점령할 수 있었다. 24일 소련군 제25군 사령관 치스차코프(I. M. Chistiakov) 대장이 선발대를 거느리고 평양에 들어왔다.

소련 점령군은 북한에 진주한 뒤 각 도의 자치위원회를 임시정치위원회로 개칭할 것을 명령하고, 이 임시정치위원회로 하여금 각 도의 치안 유지와 일제의 행정권 접수를 담당하게 하였다. 1946년 2월 5일 '북조선 각도 군, 인민대표와 반일 민주 정당 및 사회단체 회의' 를 소집하고 이 회의에서 북조선 임시인민위원회를 발족시켰다.

1946년 11월 3일 도, 시, 군 인민 위원회 선거가 처음으로 실시되었고, 다음해 1947년 2월 17일 도, 시, 군 인민 위원 대회가 평양에서 열렸다. 이 대회는 최고 입법 기관으로 북조선인민회의를 설치할 것을 결의하고 대의원을 선출하였다. 최고 입법 기관과 정권 기구가 완비된 뒤 같은 해 2월 24~25일의 동(리)인민위원회 선거와 3월 5일의 면인민위원회 선거가 실시됨으로써, 북한은 '민주 선거 방식에 의한 인민 정권 형태' 를 하부 말단에 이르기까지 완성하였다.

註釋*13 – 조선공산당(朝鮮共産黨)

1925년 4월 17일 일제하 경성부 황금정 아서원에서 조직된 사회주의 운동 단체로, 1928년 12월 해체되었다가, 1945년 8월 해방 후 박헌영(朴憲永) 등이 재조직하였으나 1946년 11월 남조선노동당(남로당)으로 해소된 정당이다.

註釋*14 – 조선민주당(朝鮮民主黨)

광복 후 평안남도건국준비위원회와 평안남도인민정치위원회의 위원장을 맡아 신망이 높던 조만식(曺晩植)이 북한 지역의 대표들과 함께 1945년 11월 3일 평양에서 결성, 창당과 동시에 당기관지인 〈조선민주보〉를 주간으로 발행하였다. 1945년 12월 말 모스크바 3상 회의 결정에 따라 신탁 통치 문제가 제기되자 조선민주당은 회의를 열어, 반탁 결의를 하고, 당수 조만식은 소련군 당국자의 신탁 통치 찬성 요청을 거부하여 연금 상태에 놓이게 됨으로써 조선민주당은 본래의 의도와는 다르게 변질되었다.

註釋*15 – 기독교사회민주당(基督敎社會民主黨)

1945년 9월 목사 윤하영(尹河英)과 한경직(韓景職) 등이 신의주(新義州)에서 결성한 정당이다.

註釋*16 – 신의주 반공 학생 의거(新義州反共學生義擧)

1945년 11월 16일 평안북도 용암포(龍巖浦)에서 열린 기독교 사회당 지방 대회에서, 평북 자치대 용암포 대표는 기념사를 통해 폐교 조치된 수산 기술학교 복구를 촉구하고, 공산당 용암포 대장 이종흡(李宗洽)의 만행을 규탄하자 이를 지지하고 나선 학생들이 만세를 외치며 '학원의 자유' 를 부르짖었다. 이에 소련군과 공산당측은 이들을 공격하였고, 평안 교회의 장로를 현장에서 사살하고, 12명의 학생 및 시민 또한 중상을 입었다.
이 소식은 신의주시 평안북도 학생 자치대 본부에 전해졌고, 격분한 신의주시의 6개 남녀 중학생들은 11월 23일 상오 9시 학교 강당에 집합하여 '공산당타도' 를 결의한 뒤 가두 행진에 나섰다. 이 사건으로 피살된 학생은 23명, 중경상자 700여 명이었고, 사건 이후 검거, 투옥된 학생과 시민은 무려 2,000여 명에 달하였다.

註釋*17 – 임정 봉대론(臨政奉戴論)
해방 직후 중경 임시 정부가 유일한 정권 수임 기관이 되어야 한다는 논리로, 한민당계 및 임정 계열 인사들이 추진한 운동이다. 해방 직후 여운형의 건국준비위원회에 참여를 제의받자 송진우는 총독부가 연합군에게 정권을 인도하기를 기다리면서, 재충칭 임시 정부를 정통으로 환영 추대할 것이라며 거절했다. 송진우는 1945년 9월 1일 '임시 정부 및 연합군 환영 준비 위원회' 를 조직하고, 임정 봉대를 주장했다.

註釋*18 – 독립촉성중앙협의회(the Independent Central Council)
1945년 10월 23일 좌, 우익을 망라한 민족 통일 기관 형성을 위해 조직된 정치 단체이다. 독립촉성중앙협의회(이하 독촉)는 1945년 10월 23일 조선 호텔에서 각 정당 대표 200명이 참석한 가운데 결성되었다. 탁치 정국하인 1946년 1월 15일 독촉은 제2회 중앙집행위원회를 개최하고, 임정 세력 중심의 비상정치회의를 흡수한다고 발표했다. 독촉을 주축으로 비상정치회의를 흡수해서 임시정부를 수립한다는 계획이었다. 1946년 1월 18일 독촉은 비상국민회의로 개칭하고 이승만에게 최고 위원 선출권을 일임했다. 반탁투쟁을 반소, 반공과 연결시키면서 임정 세력을 흡수하고자 한 것이었다. 독촉은 좌, 우익 망라, 임정 포섭 등 처음 계획에는 실패했지만, 최고 지도자로서 이승만을 부각시킨다는 프로그램에는 부응했다

註釋*19 – 이승만은 왜 공산주의를 싫어했을까?

이승만은 미국 망명 시절 프린스턴 대학교 대학원에서 국제법과 외교사를 전공했다. 1910년 6월 14일 이승만은 우드로 윌슨(Woodrow Wilson, 1856~1924) 총장으로부터 박사 학위를 받았다. 그의 '미국의 영향을 받은 중립(Neutrality as Influenced by the United States)' 이란 제목의 박사 학위 청구 논문은 1912년에 프린스턴 대학 출판부에서 출간되었다.

그리고 1914년 제1차 세계 대전이 일어나 공해상의 중립 문제가 당면 과제로 떠오르면서, 그의 논문은 학계의 관심을 끌었다. 학위를 수여한 우드로 윌슨 총장은 후에 민주당 후보로 미국 대통령에 당선되었다. 민족 자결주의로 유명한 윌슨 대통령이다. 이승만은 하바드, 프린스턴을 거치면서 공산주의 본질을 학문적으로 성찰한 정치

가였다. 공산주의에 관한 이승만의 논문과 연설에는 그의 학문적 성찰이 그대로 묻어난다.

1) 이승만의 논문 : 공산당(共産黨)의 당부당(當不當)

원문 –(가) 재산을 나누어 가지자 함이라.

모든 사람의 재산을 토지, 건축 등 모든 부동산까지 다 합해다가 평균히 나누어 차지하게 하자 함이니, 이것을 가난한 사람은 물론 환영하겠지마는, 토지를 평균히 나누어 맡긴 후에 게으른 사람들이 농사를 아니 하든지, 일을 하니 하든지 하야 토지를 다 버리게 되면 어찌 하겠느뇨? 부지런한 사람들이 부지런히 일하야 게으른 가난뱅이를 먹이어야 될 것이오, 이 가난장이는 차차 수효가 늘어서, 장차는 저마다 일 아니하고 얻어먹으려는 자가 국중(國中)에 가득할 것이며,

원문 –(나) 자본가(資本家)를 없이하자 함이라.

모든 부자의 돈을 합해다가 공동히 나누어 가지고 살게 하면 부자의 양반 노릇하는 폐단은 막히려니와, 재정가(財政家)들의 경쟁이 없어지면 상업과 공업이 발달되기 어려우니, 사람의 지혜가 막히고 모든 기기 미묘한 기계와 연장이 다 스스로 폐기되어, 지금에 이용후생(利用厚生)하는 모든 물건이 다 진보되지 못하며, 물질적 개명(開明)이 중지될지라, 자본을 철폐하기는 어려우리니, 새 법률로 제정하야 노동과 평등 세력을 가지게 하는 것이 나을 터이며,

원문 －(다) 지식 계급을 없이하자 함이니,

모든 인민의 보통 상식 정도를 높여서 지금에 학식으로 양반 노릇하는 사람들과 비등하게 되자 하는 것은 가하거니와, 지식 계급을 없이하자 함은 불가능하며,

원문 －(라) 종교 단체를 혁파하자 함이라.

자고로 종교단체가 공고히 조직되어 그 안에 인류 계급도 있고, 토지 소유권도 많으며, 이 속에서 인민 압제의 학대를 많이 했나니, 모든 구교 숭배하던 나라에서는 이 폐해를 다 알지라. 그러나 지금 새 교회의 제도는 이런 폐단도 없고 겸하야 평등, 자유의 사상이 본래 열교확장(裂教擴張)되는 중에서 발전된 것이라. 교회 조직을 없이 하는 날은 인류덕의(人類德義)상 손해가 다대할 것이며,

원문 －(마) 정부도 없고, 군사도 없으며, 국가사상도 다 없이 한다 함이라.

이에 대하야는 공산당 속에서도 이론이 많을뿐더러 지금 공산당을 주장한다는 아라사(러시아)로만 보아도, 정부와 인도자와 군사가 없이는 부지할 수 없는 사정을 자기들도 다 아는 바라, 더 설명을 요구치 않거니와 설령 세상이 다 공산당이 되며, 동서양 각국이 다 국가를 없이하여 세계적 백성을 이루며, 군사를 없이하고 총과 창을 녹여서 호미와 보습을 만들지라도, 우리 한인(韓人)은 일편단심으로 국가를 먼저 회복하야 세계에 당당한 자유국을 만들어 놓고, 군사를 길러서 우리 적국 군함이 부산 항구에 그림자도 보이지 못하게

만든 후에야, 국가주의를 없이할 문제라도 생각하지, 그 전에는 설령 국가주의를 버려서 우리 2천만이 모두 다 밀리어네어(백만장자)가 된다 할지라도 우리는 원치 아니할 지라.
우리 한민족(韓民族)에게 제일 급(急)하고, 제일 긴(緊)하고, 제일 큰 것은 광복 사업이라, 공산주의가 이를 도울 수 있으면 우리는 다 공산당이 되기를 지체치 않으려니와, 만일 이 일이 방해될 것 같으면 우리는 결코 찬성할 수 없노라.

2) 이승만의 연설문 : 공산당에 대한 나의 입장

1945년 12월 19일 저녁 7시 30분 이승만은 서울 중앙 방송국(KBS)을 통해 '공산당에 대한 나의 입장' 이라는 제목의 연설을 했다. 이 연설은 건국 지도자에 의해 이뤄진, 제2차 세계 대전 이후 공산당에 대한 세계 최초의 정면 대결 선언일 것이다.

"(공산당 극렬분자들은) '제 나라를 파괴시키고 타국의 권리 범위 내에 두어서 독립권을 영영 말살시키기로 위주하는 자' 로, 양의 무리에 이리가 섞여서 공산 명목을 빙자하고 국권을 없이하야, 나라와 동족을 팔아 사리와 영광을 위해 부언낭설로 인민을 속이며, 도당(徒黨)을 지어 동족을 위협하며, 군기(軍器)를 사용하야 재산을 약탈하며, 소위 공화국이라는 명사(名詞)를 조작하야 국민 전체의 분열 상태를 세인에게 선전하기에 이르렀더니, 요즈음은 민중이 차차 깨어나서 공산에 대한 반동이 일어나매, 간계(奸計)를 써서 각처에 선전하기를, '저희들은 공산주의자가 아니요 민족주의자' 라고 하야 민심을 현혹시키나니, 이 극렬 분자들의 목적은 우리 독립국

을 없이해서 남의 노예를 만들고, 저희 사욕(私慾)을 채우려는 것을 누구나 볼 수 있을 것이다."

"이 분자들이 러시아를 저희 조국이라 부른다니, 과연 이것이 사실이라면 우리의 요구하는 바는 이 사람들이 한국에서 떠나서, 저희 조국으로 들어가서 저희 나라를 충성스럽게 섬기라고 하고 싶다. 우리는 우리나라를 찾아서 완전히 우리 것으로 만들어 가지고, 잘하나 못하나 우리의 원하는 대로 만들어 가지고 살려는 것을, 이 사람들이 한국 사람의 형용(形容)을 하고 와서 우리 것을 빼앗아가, 저희 조국에 갖다 바치려는 것은 우리가 결코 허락지 않는 것이니, 우리 삼천만 남녀가 다 목숨을 내어놓고 싸울 결심이다."

"먼저 그 사람들을 회유해서 사실을 알려주는 것이다. 내용을 모르고 따라다니는 무리를 권유해, 돌아서게만 되면 함께 나아갈 것이요,…"

"교정이 되지 않는 공산주의자들은 '친부형(親父兄)', 친자질(親子姪)이라도 원수로 대우해야 한다. 대의를 위해서는 애증(愛憎)과 친소(親疏)를 돌아볼 수 없는 것이다."

"언제든지, 어디서든지 건설자와 파괴자는 협동이 못 되는 법이다. 건설자가 변경되든지 파괴자가 회개하든지 해서 같은 목적을 갖기 전에는 완전한 합동은 못 된다."

"이 큰 문제를 우리 손으로 해결치 못하면 종시는 다른 해방국들과 같이 나라가 두 절분(切分)으로 나뉘어져서 동족상잔의 화를 면치 못하고, 따라서 우리가 결국은 다시 남의 노예 노릇을 면하기 어려울 것이다. 그러니 우리는 경향 각처에 모든 애국 애족하는 동포의 합심 합력으로 단순한 민주정체하에 국가를 건설하야 만년 무궁한 자유복락의 기초를 세우기로 결심하자." – 손세일의 〈이승만과 김구평전〉발췌》

註釋*20 – 모스크바 3상 회의 결정서 3항의 한국관계 전문 : 코리아

(1) 코리아를 독립 국가로 재건하고 또한 민주적 원칙에 바탕을 둔 발전을 이룩할 수 있는 여건의 창출을 위하여, 그리고 장기간의 일본의 지배로 인한 참담한 결과를 가능한 빨리 제거하기 위하여, 코리아의 산업과 운수 및 농업 그리고 코리아 인의 민족 문화 발전에 필요한 모든 조치를 취할 임시적인 코리아 민주 정부를 수립할 것이다.

(2) 임시적인 코리아 정부의 구성을 돕기 위하여, 남부 코리아의 미군 사령부와 북부 코리아의 소련군 사령부의 대표들로 구성되는 공동 위원회를 설립할 것이다. 공동 위원회는 그 제안들을 준비함에 있어서 코리아의 민주적 정당-사회, 단체들과 협의할 것이다. 공동 위원회가 작성한 건의서는 공동 위원회에 대표권을 가진 양국 정부가 최종 결정을 내리기에 앞서 소련, 중국, 영국, 미국정부들의 심의를 위하여 제출되어야 한다.

(3) 임시적 코리아 민주 정부와 코리아 민주 단체들의 참여 아래, 코리아 인의 정치, 경제, 사회적 진보와 민주적인 자치 정부의 발전 및 코리아의 민족적 독립의 달성을 위하여 협력, 원조(신탁 통치)할 수 있는 방책을 작성하는 것이 공동 위원회의 임무이다. 공동 위원회의

제안은 코리아 임시 정부와 협의를 거친 후에, 최고 5년에 걸치는 코리아 4개국의 신탁에 관한 협정의 체결을 위한 미국, 소련, 영국, 중국의 공동 심의에 회부될 것이다.

(4) 남부 및 북부 코리아 모두에 영향을 미칠 긴급한 문제들을 심의하기 위하여, 그리고 행정, 경제적 문제들에 있어서의 남북 양 사령부 간의 영구적인 협력을 가능케 할 방책을 마련하기 위하여, 코리아에 있는 미국 사령부와 소련 사령부의 대표로 구성된 회의를 2주일 내로 소집할 것이다.

註釋*21 – 미소공동위원회(美蘇共同委員會)

모스크바 삼국 외상 회의의 결정에 따라 한국의 임시 정부 수립을 원조할 목적으로 미국과 소련 점령군에 의하여 설치되었던 공동 위원회다. 제2차 세계 대전의 종결 뒤 개최된 모스크바 삼국 외상 회의에서는 한국의 임시 정부 수립과 함께 미국, 영국, 중국, 소련에 의해 최장 5년간의 신탁 통치를 실시할 수 있다고 결정하였다.

또한 임시 정부 수립을 원조하고 남북 분단으로 인한 여러 문제를 해결하기 위하여 양 점령군 사이에 공동위원회를 설치할 것도 결정하였다. 이에 따라 1946～1947년 사이에 1차의 공동 회담과 2차에 걸친 미소공동위원회가 개최되었으나 미국과 소련 간의 입장 차이로 인하여 아무런 성과도 없이 무산되고 말았다.

註釋*22 - 신탁 통치(trusteeship)

국제 연합 감독 하에 시정국(施政國 : 신탁 통치를 행하는 국가)이 일정 지역(신탁 통치 지역)에 대하여 실시하는 특수 통치 제도이다. 국제 연맹이 당시 독일 및 터키에서 분리된 지역에 대하여 '위임 통치(委任統治)'를 실시했는데, 국제 연합은 이를 계승, 수정하여 신탁 통치 제도를 설치하였다. 한국은 모스크바 삼상 회의의 결의로 8·15광복 직후 5년 동안의 신탁 통치가 협의되었지만, 한국인의 반탁 운동으로 이루어지지 않았다

註釋*23 - 송진우와 여운형의 암살

1945년 12월 30일 한국민주당 수석 총무 고하(古下) 송진우(宋鎭禹) 씨를 저격한 진범인을 체포코자 경기도 경찰국에서는 약 2개 월 전부터 비밀리에 맹렬한 활동을 거듭하여 한때는 부녀 동맹 간부들도 암살 혐의를 받고 취조를 당하는 등 범인 수사의 귀추가 주목되었는데, 8일 밤부터 돌연 단서를 잡고 특별 무장 대원들이 수사를 개시하여 9일 정오까지 진범인 한원율(韓元律, 일명 韓賢宇, 29), 유근배(劉根培, 20), 김의현(金義賢, 20) 등 3명을 체포하였다.

4월 24일에 경기도 경찰부의 암살범 취조 결과 발표가 있었는데, 관계 기사에서 배경을 설명한 앞부분은 빼고 범행과 직접 관계된 뒷부분만 옮겨놓는다. 한[현우]은 도쿄 시대로부터 철저한 민족주의자인데, 해방 직후 상경하여 각 방면의 정세와 동향을 정시한즉, 자주 독립촉성을 표방하는 정당이 속출하여 자유, 해방이다 하기만 하고 통일이 안 됨을 보고 재 도쿄 시대의 동무인 이용봉(李龍鳳)의 소개로

8월 하순에 현재 시내 신당정 333의 6 경남 양산 출신 전상(全柏, 42)을 방문했다.
의견을 교환한 다음 11월 초순경에 이 두 사람은 이론 투쟁만으로는 성공할 수 없다 하여 정치적 야심가, 브로커 등을 암살 숙청할 계획을 세우고 무기를 얻는 한편, 심복 부하를 물색하여 여운형(呂運亨), 박헌영(朴憲永), 송진우(宋鎭禹) 씨 등을 매국적 행동자로 규정하고, 이상 제씨를 살해하려 하였으나 뜻대로 되지 아니하여 첫째로 신탁 문제가 일어나 격분하고 있을 즈음 12월 29일 하오 5시경 부하를 소집하고 명일 미명에 먼저 송진우를 암살할 것을 부하들에게 발표한 다음 유근배(劉根培)가 30일 상오 6시 10분경 송진우를 권총으로 암살하였다.

그리고 한은 전백의 명령을 받고 1월 3일경 서북 지방으로 반탁을 선전하러 갔다가 1월 17일 서울에 돌아왔는데, 그 후로 여운형과 박헌영의 거소를 찾고 있었다. 주범들은 공산주의자라고는 인정할 수 없다.
– 서울신문 (1946. 04. 24.)

한현우 등이 재판시 진술에서 '송진우는 미국의 후견을 지지했다'는 주장은 12월 29일 밤 경교장 회의에서 송진우의 발언 내용을 의미하는 것이다. 송건호는 한현우를 국수적 민족주의 광신자라고 평가했다. 한현우의 송진우 암살은 대한민국 임시 정부 특파 사무국의 후신인 백의사가 배후인 것으로 추정되고 있다.

당초부터 '반공'을 강하게 내걸었던 백의사(白衣社)는 공산주의자들은 물론 그들과 협력하는 정치인들도 제거 대상이었다. 여운형도 그 중 하나였다. 1947년 7월 19일 혜화동 거리에서 여운형을 암살한 사람은 한지근(본명 이필형)이라는 19세 젊은이였다(실제 나이는 25세였다고 함).

한지근의 배후에는 격몽의숙(擊蒙義塾)이라는 극우(極右)조직이 있었다. 격몽의숙의 리더는 송진우(宋鎭禹) 암살 사건의 주범인 한현우(韓賢宇)였다. 송진우 암살 사건으로 한현우가 감옥에 갇힌 뒤에는 그의 추종자인 신동운이 격몽의숙을 이끌면서, 한지근 등 오갈 데 없는 젊은이들을 교육했다. 한현우는 1993년 2월 21일자 《한겨레》와의 인터뷰에서 이렇게 주장했다.

"당시 신탁 통치를 했을 경우, 여운형을 주석으로 시키려고 했었다. 여운형을 주석으로 삼았다면 한국은 적화되고 말았을 것이다. 나는 공산주의와 김일성을 막기 위해서는 신탁 통치를 해서는 안 된다고 생각해, 감방에 면회 온 동지들에게 여운형을 살해하라는 지령도 내렸다."

한현우의 지시에 따라 여운형 암살을 모의하던 신동운, 김흥성 등을 염동진과 연결시켜 준 사람은 백의사 고문 김영철이었다. 당시 60대 초이던 김영철은 김구의 한인 애국단에서 활동했다는 인물이었다. 염동진은 "여운형은 민족 분열을 조장하는 야심가"라면서 이들에게 45구경 권총을 건네주었다.

여운형 암살범들은 또 다른 극우조직인 혁신탐정사의 양근환(일제시대 친일 언론인 민원식을 암살한 독립 운동가)으로부터도 일제 99

식 권총을 받았다. 여운형의 목숨을 끊은 것은 염동진이 준 미제 45구경 권총이었다.

註釋*24 – 신탁통치반대국민총동원위원회(信託統治反對國民總動員委員會)

신탁통치반대국민총동원위원회는 김구를 비롯한 임시 정부 진영이 적극적이고 조직적인 신탁 통치 반대 활동을 펼치려는 목적에서 결성한 것이다.

임시 정부 측은 모스크바 삼상 회의(1945. 12. 16.～27.)의 결정에 따라 한반도에 미소 공동 위원회를 설치하고, 미소 공동 위원회가 한반도의 신탁 통치안을 협의한다는 소식이 전해지자, 1945년 12월 28일 긴급 국무 회의를 열고 이어서 각 정당, 종교 단체, 언론 기관 대표들을 초청하여 비상 대책 회의를 개최하였는데, 이 자리에서 신탁통치반대국민총동원위원회의 구성을 결의하였다.

1945년 12월 29일, 중앙 위원 회의를 열어서 임시 정부의 즉각적 주권 행사를 건의하였다. 12월 31일에는 전국적 총파업을 지시하기도 하였다. 1946년 2월 8일 이승만이 지도하는 독립촉성중앙협의회(지방 단위들)와 통합하여 대한독립촉성국민회로 재편되었다.

註釋*25 – 국자(國字) **1호와 2호 포고문**

국자(國字) 1호

(1) 현재 전국 행정청 소속의 경찰 기구 및 한인 직원은 전부 본 임시 정부 지휘 하에 예속케 함.

(2) 신탁 반대의 시위 운동은 계통적 질서적으로 행할 것.
(3) 폭력 행위와 파괴 행위는 절대금지 함.
(4) 국민의 최저 생활에 필요한 식량, 연료, 수도, 전기, 교통, 금융, 의료 기관 등의 확보 운영에 대한 방해를 금지함.
(5) 불량 산인의 폭리 매점 등은 취체함.

국자(國字) 2호

차운동은 반드시 우리의 최후 승리를 획득할 때까지 계속함을 요하며, 우리 국민은 금후 우리 정부 지도하에 제반 산업을 부흥하기를 요망한다.

註釋*26 – 비상정치회의주비회(非常政治會議籌備會)

비상정치회의주비회는 임시 정부가 임정 법통론에 입각하여 소집, 구성한 예비 입법 기구이자 통일 전선체였다. 김구는 1946년 1월 4일, 3단계 정부 수립 방안과 함께 비상정치회의의 소집을 공표하였다. 그에 따르면 우선 임시 정부를 확대, 강화하고, 곧 구성될 비상정치회의를 통해서 과도 정부를 수립(임시 정부를 해체)하고, 과도 정부 아래 민주 정신에 따라 국민 대표 대회를 소집하여 정식 독립 정부를 구성한다는 것이었다.

註釋*27 – 조선노동조합전국평의회(朝鮮勞動組合全國評議會)

약칭 '전평(全評)' 이라고 한다. 1945년 11월 5일 전국 각지로부터 505명의 대의원이 참석한 가운데 결성되었다. 그리하여 조선노동조합 전국 평의회는 조선민주청년동맹(朝鮮民主青年同盟)의 청년 조직과 더불어 조선공산당의 양대 세력이 되었던 단체였다. 전평은 조선인민공화국 지지, 찬탁 운동 참여, 9월 총파업 등으로 미 군정에 대한 적대관계를 분명히 함으로써 결국 극좌 정치 운동으로 나아갔다

註釋*28 – 비상국민회의(非常國民會議)

임시 정부가 1945년 9월 충칭(重慶)에서 발표한 임시 정부 당면 정책 제6항에 따라 임시 정부를 중심으로 국내외 각계 각층 대표를 소집, 비상 정치 회의를 열어 과도 정권을 수립한 뒤에 다시 국민대표대회를 소집하여 헌법을 제정, 정식 정부를 수립하자는 것이었다. 이렇게 함으로써 신탁 통치를 사실상 배제하자는 것이었다.

1월 20일부터 24일까지 5일 간 비상정치회의의 제1차 주비 회의(籌備會議)를 개최하였다. 이 회의에서는 이승만(李承晩)의 독립촉성중앙협의회(獨立促成中央協議會)와 비상정치회의를 합류시키기로 결정하고, 명칭을 '비상국민회의' 로 바꾸어 이승만과 김구를 영수로 추대하였다.

註釋*29 – 대한국민대표민주의원(大韓國民代表民主議院)

1946년 2월 1일과 2일 임시 정부측 주최로 과도 정부 수립을 목적으로 소집된 비상 국민 회의가 그 의결로써 28명의 최고 정무 위원을 선출하였던 바, 미 군정의 종용을 받아 주한미군사령관 하지(Hodge, J. R.)의 자문 기관으로서 과도 정부 수립을 촉진시키는 사명을 띠고 2월 14일 설치되었다.

註釋*30 – 철의 장막(iron curtain)

처칠(Winston Leonard Spencer churchill) 영국 총리가 1946년 3월 5일에 미국을 방문하였을 때 미주리 주의 풀턴에서 트루먼(Harry S. Truman) 대통령의 배석 하에 이루어진 연설에서 사용한 소련에 의한 동 유럽 지배의 비유, 또는 소련 진영의 국가들의 폐쇄성을 풍자한 말이다. 이 연설에서 처칠은 발트 해에 면한 수데텐란트에서 남으로 내려와 아드리아 해에 면한 트리에스테까지의 선상(線上)에 '철의 장막' 이 쳐져 있다고 하여 소련에 의한 동 유럽 지배를 비판하였다.

원래 동유럽 국가는 제2차 세계대전 중에는 나치 독일군에게 점령되거나 그 동맹국이 되었지만, 1943년 1월 스탈린그라드의 전투에서 소련군이 승리한 이래 독일군의 철수와 함께 소련군에 의해 해방되었다. 또한 1945년 2월의 알타회담에서 합의된 '해방 유럽에 관한 선언' 에 따라 전후의 동유럽에는 공산당뿐만 아니라 다른 반(反)파시즘 정당을 포함한 연합 정권이 수립되었다.

그럼에도 불구하고 처칠이 소련에 의한 동유럽 지배라고 비판한 배경에는 소련의 위협적인 강요로 미국과의 동맹을 강화하고 영국에서의 자신의 정치적 영향력을 회복하기 위한 의도가 있었지만 결과적으로 미소 냉전의 예고적인 연설이 되었다.

註釋*31 – 한국민주당(韓國民主黨)

약칭 '한민당' 이라고 한다. 1945년 9월 16일 서울 천도교 기념관에서 발기인 1,600여 명이 모여 창당 대회를 가졌다. 이에 참석한 정당, 단체는 고려민주당, 조선민족당, 한국국민당, 국민대회준비회, 충칭

(重慶) 임시 정부 및 연합군 환영 준비위원회 등이었다.
이들 정당, 단체를 대표하는 민족지도자들은 1945년 9월 4일 서울 종로국민학교에서 대표 82명이 모여 신당 발기 총회를 가지고 당명을 '한국민주당' 으로 결정하였으며, 9월 8일에는 한국민주당 발기인 1,000여 명 명의로 조선인민공화국 타도 성명서를 발표하고, 충칭 임시 정부 절대지지 태도를 밝혔다.

註釋*32 – 코뮤니케 제5호

1946년 3월 20일, 서울에서 제1차 미소공동위원회가 개최됨에 따라 모스크바 결정에 의한 신탁 통치를 반대해 오던 우익 및 민족진영은 처지가 미묘하게 되었다. 이에 민주 의원의 의장인 이승만은 사의를 표명하였다. 민주 의원의 만류로 유보되었으나 민주 의원의 활동을 부진 상태에 빠져들었다. 4월 17일 미소공동위원회의 협의 대상이 되려면 모스크바 협정을 지지하는 선언서에 서명을 해야 한다는 이른바 미소공동위원회 '코뮤니케 제5호' 가 발표되었다. 반탁 진영에서는 즉각 거부의 뜻을 비추었으나 미 군정청의 하지 중장의 강력한 설득과 종용으로 5월 1일 일제히 선언서를 제출하였다. 반탁 진영의 주장은, 선언서 제출이 신탁 통치를 수락하는 것은 아니며 오히려 반탁 민족 진영이 미소공동위원회를 통한 임시 통일 정부 수립에 참가함으로써 신탁통치를 실질적으로 반대할 수 있는 계기가 된다는 것이었다.

註釋*33 – 정읍 발언(井邑發言)

1945년 12월, 모스크바 3상 회의의 결정에 따라 미국과 소련의 임시 정부 수립을 위해 개최된 제1차 미소공동위원회가 결렬되자, 미 군정이 남한만의 단독 정부 수립을 계획하고 있다는 소식이 국내에 보도되었다. 좌익 중심의 찬탁 운동과 우익 중심의 반탁 운동의 대결이 극심해지는 가운데 1946년 6월 3일, 각지를 순회하는 도중 이승만은 정읍에서

"이제 우리는 무기 휴회된 공위가 재개될 기색도 보이지 않으며, 통일 정부를 고대하나 여의케 되지 않으니, 우리는 남방만이라도 임시 정부, 혹은 위원회 같은 것을 조직하여 38 이북에서 소련을 철퇴하도록 세계 공론에 호소하여야 될 것이다."

라는 정치적 발언을 했다. 이 발언 이후, 이승만은 남한 단독 정부 수립에 본격적으로 나섰고, 그 해 12월부터 1947년 4월까지 미국에 건너가 남한 단독 정부 수립을 촉구하는 외교 활동을 벌이고 돌아왔다. 그러나 소련 붕괴 이후 공개된 소련 정부의 기록, 특히 스탈린의 북한에 대한 지시 자료를 검토한 일부 학자들은 스탈린의 북한 단독 정부 수립 계획은 이승만의 발언 이전부터 진행되고 있었다고 주장하기도 한다.

註釋*34 – 조선정판사 위폐 사건(朝鮮精版社僞幣事件)

1945년 8 · 15광복 이후 여러 정치 세력들이 난립하고 있는 상황에서 조선공산당은 일제가 조선은행권을 인쇄하던 근택(近澤) 빌딩을 접수하여 조선정판사로 개칭하고, 이를 위조지폐 발행 장소로 사용하

였다. 그들은 재정난으로 인하여 당 활동 자금 조달 방책을 모색하고 있던 중 조선정판사에 지폐 원판이 있다는 것을 알고 당원인 박낙종 사장에게 그들의 계획을 알렸다. 박낙종은 같은 곳에서 근무하던 공산당원 김창선(金昌善)에게 당 재정부장 이관술(李觀述)과 당 중앙 집행 위원이며 해방일보사 사장인 권오직(權五稷)의 지령을 전하였다.

1945년 10월 20일, 서울시 소공동 74번지에 있는 근택 빌딩 내 조선정판사 사장실에서 사장 박낙종, 서무과장 송언필(宋彦弼), 재무과장 박정상(朴鼎相), 기술과장 김창선, 평판기술공 정명환(鄭明煥), 창고계주임 박창근(朴昌根) 등이 비밀리에 모여 위조 지폐를 인쇄, 공산당에 제공할 것을 결의하였다. 그리하여 그날 오후 7시 공장 종업원들이 퇴근한 뒤 김창선이 평판과장으로 있을 때 절취, 보관하고 있던 100원권 원판(징크판) 등으로 모두 여섯 차례에 걸쳐 위조 지폐 1,200만 원을 위조하여 이관술에게 제공, 공산당의 활동비로 사용하게 하였다.

출처 불명의 위조 지폐가 나돌아 경제를 혼란시키자 경찰은 수사에 착수하여 김창선이 지폐원판 1매를 서울오프셋인쇄소 윤석현(尹奭鉉)에게 보관시킨 것을 탐지하고 범인 체포에 나서 1946년 5월 4일과 5일 중부경찰서(당시 本町경찰서) 형사대가 이재원 등 일당 7명을 체포하였다. 이어 그들의 자백에 의하여 5월 7일 공산당원 16명 중 간부 3명을 제외한 14명을 체포하였다.

註釋*35 – 신전술(新戰術)

조선공산당은 해방 이후 미 군정에 대해 직접적인 비난이나 적대 행위를 자제했던 자세에서 벗어나, 1946년 7월 이후 적극적인 투쟁과 물리적 저항에 나서게 되었다. 이때 채택한 전술이 '신전술' 이다. 이것은 미 군정과 남한의 우익을 차별해 대응하는 '이중전술' 을 핵심으로 한다. 조선공산당은 미 군정에 대해서는 '공세적 압박 전술' 을 사용하고, 남한 내의 우익 세력에 대해서는 '정당 방위의 자위 전술' 이라는 성격으로 전술을 구체화했다.

공세적 압박과 정당방위의 자위 전술은 이후 9월 총파업과 10월 항쟁 등으로 이어졌고, 이는 신전술의 정책 방향 아래 이루어진 것이었다. 신전술은 대중들의 불만과 요구의 해결책으로 제기되는 민주개혁의 과제가 북한에서는 이미 시행되고 있음을 선전함으로써 남한에서 조선공산당의 지지를 회복하고, 이를 바탕으로 미 군정에 대한 공세적 압박을 통해 미소공위를 재개시키려는 의도를 가지고 있었다.

註釋*36 – 영구차 행렬로 위장한 박헌영의 월북

정판사 위조 지폐 사건은 당시 제1차 미소공동위원회가 무기 휴회로 들어간 상태(1946. 05. 8.)에서 미 군정이 좌익에 대하여 본격적으로 탄압을 시작하게 된 직접적 계기가 되었다. 1946년 9월 6일, 박헌영을 비롯한 조선공산당 간부 이강국, 이주하에게 체포령이 발부되었다. 같은 날 미 군정청은 3대 좌익 신문 조선인민보, 중앙신문, 현대일보를 폐간시키고, 신문사의 간부들을 체포했다. 이때 박헌영은 지하로 잠입했다가 북한으로 탈출했다.

박헌영의 월북 시기에 관한 여러 엇갈린 견해들이 있다. 하나는, "미 군정의 체포령이 떨어지기 전날인 1946년 9월 5일 오전 8시, 관 속에 들어가 장례차로 위장하여 의정부 포천 위쪽 양문리 근처 38선에서 이동수 외 5명 청년들의 경호를 받으면서 이북 해주로 탈출했다."는 견해이다. 박갑동 씨는 그의 저서 〈박헌영〉167～168쪽에서 "박헌영은 1946년 9월 6일 체포령 전에 극적으로 서울에서 극비리에 탈출했다."라고 기록하였다.

그리고 그의 탈출 행각에 대해서, "박헌영은 이 날 한 평 반 남짓한 영구차 속, 자기키보다 조금 큰 검은 관 속에 반듯이 누워 시체를 가장해서 월북했다. 38선 접경에 이를 때까지 혹시나 경찰의 검문을 염려해서 가족으로 분장한 남녀 당원 몇몇이 흡사 경기도 일원의 어느 선산에 매장이나 하러 가는 듯한 장례 차림을 꾸민 것이다. … 이 행렬에 뽑힌 5명의 호위원은 공산당 내에서 엄선된 일당백의 행동 대원들이었다." 라고 자세히 기록하였다.

註釋*37 – 좌우합작위원회(左右合作委員會)

1946년 5월경 국내 정치 세력은 미 군정의 분류 기준에 따르자면 이승만(李承晩), 김구(金九)를 중심으로 하는 극우세력, 김규식, 원세훈 등의 중도 우파 세력, 여운형을 중심으로 하는 중도 좌파 세력, 박헌영(朴憲永)을 중심으로 하는 극좌 세력으로 나누어져 있었다. 이러한 상황 속에서 좌익 탄압과 함께 우익 세력 강화를 도모할 수 있는 유력한 방법으로 선택된 미국의 정책이었다.

註釋*38 – 10월항쟁(十月抗爭)

1946년 10월 2일 대구에서 발생한 경찰과 시민들 간의 대규모 유혈 충돌. 10월 1일 파업에 대한 군, 경, 테러단의 폭행에 항의하는 군중 집회에 경찰이 발포, 사망자가 발생하자, 다음날 노동자, 시민, 학생이 합세하여 경찰관서를 습격함으로써 시작되었다. 이에 대구 지역에는 계엄령이 선포되었으나, 미 군정과 경찰에 대항하는 격렬한 시위는 성주, 고령, 영천, 경산 등지로 번져 나갔으며, 경남, 전남, 전북, 강원 등 전국으로 퍼졌다.

초기의 총파업은 전평의 지휘 하에 이루어졌으나, 이후 전국 각지에서 발생한 민중들의 항쟁은 이미 공산당의 통제를 떠나 민중들의 쌓인 불만이 격렬하게 터져 나온 것이었다. 이 사건으로 각지의 경찰서, 파출소, 면사무소가 파괴되고 수많은 희생자가 발생했다. 9월 총파업과 10월 항쟁의 결과, 공산당은 큰 타격을 입었으며, 잔존하던 지방의 인민위원회도 철저히 파괴되었다.

註釋*39 – 남조선노동당(南朝鮮勞動黨)**, 약칭 남로당**(南勞黨)

좌익 세력을 총집결하기 위하여 여운형(呂運亨)이 당수로 있던 조선인민당(朝鮮人民黨) 및 백남운(白南雲)이 당수로 있던 남조선신민당(南朝鮮新民黨)과의 3당 합당 공작에 착수하였다. 1946년 9월 4일에는 3당 합동 준비 위원회 연석회의가 개최되었다. 합당 결정서와 선언 및 강령이 채택되었으며, 남조선노동당준비위원회가 구성되었다. 1946년 11월 23일 박헌영과 그의 지지파는 '남조선노동당' 을 결성하였다.

註釋*40 – 남조선과도입법의원(南朝鮮過渡立法議院)

1946년 5월 6일, 제1차 미소공동위원회가 무기 휴회되자 미 군정 당국은 김규식(金奎植), 여운형(呂運亨) 등 온건한 좌우파의 지도자들에게 좌우 합작 운동을 적극 알선하는 한편, 이들을 중심으로 과도입법 의원을 구성하였다.

1946년 6월 29일, 군정장관 러치(Lerche, A. L.)는 조선 인민이 요구하는 법령을 조선 인민의 손으로 제정하는 입법 기관의 창설을 미군 사령관 하지(Hodge, J. R.)에게 건의하여 그 해 7월 9일 하지의 동의를 얻어 8월 24일 남조선과도입법의원의 창설을 발표하게 하였다. 입법의원은 모스크바 삼상 회의 협정에 의한 통일임시정부가 수립될 때까지 정치적 · 경제적 · 사회적 개혁의 기초로 사용될 법령 초안을 작성하는 임무를 갖고 있었다.

註釋*41 – 트루먼 독트린(Truman Doctrine)

1947년 3월, 미국 대통령 트루먼이 의회에서 선언한 미국 외교 정책에 관한 원칙이다. 그 요지는 공산주의 세력의 확대를 저지하기 위하여 자유와 독립의 유지에 노력하며, 소수자의 정부 지배를 거부하는 의사를 가진 여러 나라에 대하여 군사적 · 경제적 원조를 제공한다는 것이었다.

이 원칙에 입각하여 당시 공산세력으로 인하여 직접적인 위협에 직면하고 있던 그리스와 터키의 반공(反共) 정부에 대하여 미국의 경제적 · 군사적 원조가 제공되었다. 이 원칙은 그 후 미국 외교 정책의 기조가 되었으며, 유럽 부흥 계획과 북대서양 조약으로써 구체화

되어 갔다

註釋*42 - 격몽의숙

평안북도 영변 출신인 한지근은 서울로 내려왔지만 번번한 벌이가 없어 경제적으로 매우 어려움을 겪고 있었다. 같은 영변 출신으로 먼저 월남한 중학 동창 김훈을 찾아가자 그는 숙식이 가능한 집을 소개해 주었다. 집은 '격몽의숙' 이라고 자칭했고 집주인은 송진우 암살범으로 극우 테러 조직을 이끌던 한현우였다. 감옥에 있는 한현우를 대신해 백의사를 유지하며 집에 기거하던 인물은 신동운이었다. 신동운은 송진우의 경호원이었다.

신동운은 파시즘 내용이 다분한 한현우의 옥중수기를 한지근에게 읽도록 권유하며 민족의 분열을 유도하는 자들을 처단하는 것이 애국이라는 논리를 주입시켰다. 신동운은 한현우의 결심공판에 한지근을 데려가는 등 테러요원으로 양성했다. 한지근은 신동운이 지어준 가명이었다. 여운형 암살은 한지근의 단독 범행이라고 발표되었다. 하지만 1974년 김흥성, 김영성, 김훈, 유용호 4명이 자신들이 배후라고 공개 기자 회견을 열었다. 공소 시효가 지난 탓에 이들에 대한 조사와 처벌도 이뤄지지 않았다

註釋*43 - 백의사(白衣社)

백의사는 염응택의 주도로 1945년 11월 서울에서 월남한 청년, 학생들을 중심으로 조직되어 북한 지역과 남한 지역에서 공히 활동한 극우 반공 테러 공작단이다. '백의사(白衣社)' 라는 명칭은 중국 국민

당 정부의 반공 지하 공작 단체인 남의사(藍衣社)를 모방한 것이다. 1945년 9월 조선공산당 평안남도 도위원장 현준혁을 암살한 것으로 알려진 대동단이 백의사의 전신이고 염응택, 박고봉, 백관옥, 선우봉, 박진양 등이 대동단의 주요 인물들이다. 백의사는 현준혁 암살 사건 직후 대동단의 관련자들이 월남하여 개칭, 정비한 동일 성격의 단체이다.

백의사는 반공, 반탁, 반북을 기치로 한 대북 테러, 암살, 첩보 활동을 전개하였다. 첩보원들을 훈련시켜 북한 지역에 파견하였고 파견된 요원들은 토지 개혁 반대 선동, 신탁 통치 반대 활동, 주요 지도자 및 조직, 단체에 대한 정보 수집, 임시 정부지지 활동 등을 전개하였다. 그리고 임시 정부 내무상 신익희가 조직한 정치 공작대와 협력하여 김일성 암살 시도(1946년 3월 1일), 최용건 자택 습격(1946년 3월 5일, 7일), 김책 자택 습격(1946년 3월 9일), 강양욱 자택 습격(1946년 3월 12일) 등을 감행하였다.

백의사는 남한 지역에서도 동일한 반공 활동을 폈는데, 특히 장덕수와 여운형의 암살을 행한 것으로 알려져 있다. 그 외에도 경찰과 국방 경비대, 노동 총연맹 등에 구성원들을 가입시켜 활동하도록 하였다. 백의사는 미군 방첩대(CIC)의 지원을 받아 대북 첩보, 정보 활동을 수행하기도 하였다. 이러한 관계는 대한민국 정부수립 이후에 지속되었고 한국전쟁을 계기로 백의사의 성원 상당수가 미극동군사령부 주한연락사무소(KLO: Korea Liaison Office) 부대로 흡수되었다.

註釋*44 – 장덕수의 암살

1947년 12월 2일 오후 6시 50분경, 우익 민족진영의 최고 이론가 설산(雪山) 장덕수가 제기동 자택에서 손님들과 환담을 나누던 중 종로 경찰서 소속 경찰관 박광옥과 공범 배희범이 쏜 총탄을 맞고 자택에서 숨졌다. 이때 붙잡힌 배희범, 박광옥 등과 그들의 배후로 지목된 김석황은 모두 한국독립당 소속이었고, 김석황은 한독당 중앙위원이자 국민회의 동원부장, 임시 정부 등에도 관여하였다.

용의자 6명은 장덕수를 암살할 목적으로 1947년 8월 창단된 대한혁명단을 조직하였는데, 이들은 임정을 절대 지지하는 대한학생총연맹의 간부 또는 맹원들이기도 했다. 대한학생총연맹은 1947년 6월 운현궁에서 발족되었는데 김구를 총재, 조소앙과 엄항섭을 명예위원장으로 추대하였다. 박광옥은 종로 경찰서의 경사로 근무하는 경찰관이었고, 배희범은 초등학교 교사로 모두 한독당 당원이었다.

註釋*45 – 한국 문제의 UN 상정 및 총선거 결의

남북한 문제해결을 위한 미소공동위원회 활동이 무산되자, 미국은 1947년 9월 '한국 독립' 문제를 제2차 유엔 정기총회에 안건으로 제출하였다. 이 안건에 대해 유엔총회 운영위원회에서 소련과 폴란드는 반대, 타이완(臺灣)과 영국 등은 찬성하였다.

註釋*46 – UN 한국임시위원단

UN 총회는 1947년 11월 14일, 본회의에서 전국적인 총선거를 통해 한국에 독립 정부를 수립하기로 결의함과 동시에 이 목적을 달성하기 위한 UN 한국임시위원단(Theunited Nations Temporary Commission on Korea)을 구성했다.

註釋*47 – 남북 협상의 과정(남북 요인 회담)

1948년 2월 중간파 정치 세력인 민족자주연맹은 위원장 김규식의 주재로 정치 위원 홍명희(洪命憙), 원세훈(元世勳) 등 5명과 안재홍(安在鴻), 여운홍(呂運弘), 최동오(崔東旿), 유석현(劉錫鉉), 이상백(李相佰) 등 상무 위원 17명이 김규식의 숙소 삼청장에서 연석 회의를 열고 북한의 김일성(金日成), 김두봉(金枓奉)에게 남북 요인회담 개최를 요망하는 서신을 보내기로 결의, 한국독립당 위원장 김구의 승낙을 얻어 김구, 김규식 두 사람의 연서로 보내기로 합의하였다.

이에 따라 엄항섭(嚴恒燮)이 기초한 남북 요인 회담 개최 요망서가 서울 주재 소련군 대표부를 통하여 북한에 전달되었다. 국제연합임시위원단의 인도 대표 K.메논과 중국 대표 리우위완[劉馭萬]은 이에 관심을 보이면서 북한측 회답이 오는 대로 국제연합 소총회에 반영하려고 하였으나, 북한으로부터 아무런 회답이 없었기 때문에 국제연합소총회는 미국 대표의 제안에 따라 메논의 제1방안, 즉 총선거는 가능한 지역인 남한에서만 추진한다는 방안이 31:2로 가결됨으로써 분단의 비극이 시작되었다.

이 결정은 단독 정부 수립을 추진하던 한국민주당과 대한독립촉성국민대회를 비롯한 정당 단체 대표들에게는 희소식이었으나, 김구 등 통일 정부 수립을 갈망하던 중도 세력에게는 실망을 안겨주었다.

북한은 4월 14일부터 평양에서 남한의 모든 민주주의 정당사회단체

회의를 개최하여 조선의 민주주의 독립 국가 건설을 이룩하자는 내용의 북한민주주의민족통일전선 제26차 중앙위원회의 결정을 평양 방송과 서신으로 남한의 17개 정당사회단체 및 김구, 김규식 등 15명에게 전달하였다.

이 제의는 김구와 김규식이 보낸 서신에 대해서는 아무 언급도 없다가 국제연합 결의에 의하여 남한 단독 정부 수립이 기정사실화되자 나온 점에서 알 수 있듯이, 남한 측의 정부 수립 노선의 정당성을 약화시키고 북한 측의 입장을 정당화하려는 방편이었다. 그럼에도 불구하고 통일을 갈망하는 국민들의 기대가 컸기 때문에, 김구와 김규식은 그 동안 남북 간에 오고간 서신을 공개하면서 두 사람이 남북 요인 회담을 요청한 이상 가는 것이 옳다고 본다는 자신들의 입장을 밝혔다.

註釋*48 - 소련외무성소관문제 - 1948.1.21.
소련대외정책고문서보관소 문서번호 F07,OP.21.P22.D.316

註釋*49 - 비신스키, 몰로토프동지에게 비준바람 - 1948.4.19.
소련대외정책고문서보관소-문서번호 NO.88/MA)

註釋*50 - 레베데프 비망록 18쪽

註釋*51 - 레베데프 비망록 20쪽

註釋*52 - 4월17일자 레베데프 비망록

註釋*53 - 레베데프 비망록 52쪽

註釋*54 – 경향신문 1948년 4월 17일 기사

註釋*55 – 전조선 정당사회단체 대표자 연석회의

1948년 4월 19일, 남북 제정당 사회단체 대표자 연석회의 본회의가 남북 46개 단체 대표 545명이 참석한 가운데 평양에서 개최되었다. 김일성의 사회로 진행된 이 날 회의는, 조선의 정치 정세 및 남한 단선, 단정 반대 투쟁 대책을 회의 안건으로 채택했다.

註釋*56 – 북한의 헌법 제정

사회 경제 개혁과 권력 구조의 정비, 민족간부 양성 등을 통해 국가 건설의 기초를 닦은 북한의 사회주의 세력은 이런 성과를 바탕으로 국가의 기초를 성문화하는 헌법 마련에 나섰다. 1948년 3월에 개최될 예정이었던 임시 헌법 채택을 위한 인민회의가 4월로 연기되었다. 북한만의 헌법 논의가 남북 협상에 부정적인 영향을 미칠까 우려했기 때문으로 보인다.

남북 제정당 사회단체 대표자 연석회의가 종료된 뒤인 1948년 4월 29일, 북조선 인민회의 특별 회의는 헌법 초안을 만장 일치로 채택했다. 대표자 연석회의에 이어 남북 제정당 사회단체 지도자협의회가 열리고 있는 도중이었다. 김일성은 이 헌법이 남북한 인민 모두가 찬성을 한 헌법이라고 선전했다.

어둠에서 빛으로 가는 방황의 길

– 고산지 서사시《독립 없는 해방은 시리도록 아프다》

채수영(시인, 문학비평가)

1. 역사와 서사시

메소포타미아 티그리스 강 변에 우르크(Uruk)를 126년 동안 통치했던 왕 길가메시(Gilgamesh)는 약 4800년 전쯤의 서사시《길가메시》의 일대기를 점성토로 기록했고, 중국에서는 죽간竹簡으로, 유럽에서는 파피루스(papyrus)로 인류 문화의 기록이 시작되었다. 서사시《길가메시》이후 약 2천 년 뒤에 호머의《일리아드》,《오디세이》가 나왔고, 그 이후로 문학의 태동은 갈래를 형성하면서 오늘에 이르렀다.

장구한 세월 동안 남자의 전유물인 pen에서 1940년 이후 컴퓨터의 변화는 경천동지驚天動地의 문화를 구축하는 지경에 이르렀다. 2029년이면 AI가 인간의 지능에 접근하고, 2045년이면 로봇이 인간을 앞서는 특이점에 도달한다는 예언은 우리 앞에 서 있다.

이런 문화의 발달 추세는 결국 인간의 삶에 대한 변화를 전제로 한다. 기계와 인간의 역사가 공존으로 접어들었고, 여기서 과거와는 다른 형태의 생활 진전이 예상된다. 다시 말해서 인간의 역사는 곧 문학의 소재가 되고, 이 소재의 바탕은 다시 삶의 변화를 수용하는 쪽으로 갈래를 형성할 것이다. 또한, 서사시는 곧 역사 속에 있었던 인물이나 사건을 시적 상상의 옷을 입을 때 비로소 문학으로의 표정을 감지하게 된다. 그 때문에 역사는 곧 문학의 바탕을 구성하는 절대 인자因子로 불가분의 관계망을 설정하게 된다.

2. 문학과 서사시

서사시의 구축은 영웅의 일대기였고, 이로부터 소설이 길을 개척하게 된다. 18세기 산업혁명 이후 소설은 비로소 인간의 리얼한 현상을 묘사나 설명으로 혹은 심리적 방법으로 인간문화의 한 굴대를 감당해 왔다. 그러나 소설은 미구에 소설가가 쓰는 것이 아니라 과학자 혹은 비전문가에 의해 만들어질 것을 예고한다. 줄거리를 입력하면 한 편의 소설을 써 내는 시대로 접어들었다.

〈조선일보〉 (2018. 08. 11.)에 '비서와 CEO' 키 워드를 주니 AI가 로맨스 소설을 완성했다는 기사에는 산업경영공학과 박사 과정의 학생이고, 3,600자 소설을 단 1초에 완성했다는 보도는 이제 시나리오나 소설의 구조는 인간의 곁을 떠나고 있음을 의미한다. 문학의 땅에도 변화가 몰아친다는 것을 의미하기 때문이다. 그렇다면 문학에도 상상의 산물이라야 살아남을 수 있다는 예상은 새로운 현상이 아니다.

우리의 과거 문화는 《사서삼경》의 주석註釋이나 외우는 지식의 한계로, 중국 역사인 《25사》나 《자치통감》 혹은 《통감절》를 배우고 외우는 일에 집착하여 우리의 역사는 뒷전이었으니, 문학의 꽃인 시詩 또한 《시경詩經》 305수에 매달려 우리의 정서를 창조로 연결한 것은 거의 없었다. 이는 앞사람의 문화를 금과옥조로 떠받들면서 오로지 창조보다는 선대의 문화를 '계승繼承' 하는 것을 학문으로 알았기 때문에 문학에서도 위대한 창작 문학– 비극을 겪었어도 〈서부 전선 이상 없다〉와 같은 전쟁문학이 없고 뛰어난 연애 소설이 없다.

다시 말해서 선인들의 문학에 대한 계승을 절대의 가치로 신봉하는 풍조는 상상想像의 차단을 가져왔고, 이런 이유로 《시경》은 시에 절대적인 교과서- 벽을 넘지 못한 마치, 시의 전범典範처럼 신봉했던 것을 반성할 필요는 없을까. '사서삼경' 에 주석註釋을 다는 것으로써 오로지 학문의 본질로 생각한 우리 문화의 특성은 우리만의 것에 부재를 가져왔다.

서사시의 경우, 《용비어천가》나 《월인천강지곡》 등 특수 분야에 한정하는 표현의 빈약성을 노증했으니, 이런 현상은 결국 상상력의 고갈 풍조, 즉 문학의 바탕에 찬양가에 한정하는 것은 우리 학문의 풍조가 만든 반성의 목록일 것 같다.

3. 현대사 그리고 서사시

일제 36년은 우리 민족에게는 암흑기라 칭한다. 주권이 침탈되었고 자주권이 상실된 것은 결국 우리 자신의 유약한 역사적인 현상을 지적하게 된다. 왜냐하면, 역사의 최종 책임은 곧 그 국민의 몫이기 때문이다. 조선 말기의 풍조는 외세의 침탈 앞에 아무런 대비도 없었던 사실이 곧 암흑기를 가져오는 길이었기 때문이다.

왕조의 몰락뿐만 아니라 정신精神의 몰락을 가져온 근원은 지도자들의 어긋난 판단에서 미래를 위한 대비를 소홀히 한 죄명은 당연한 사실이다. 하여, 36년의 질곡桎梏의 세월은 참담한 비명을 삼키는 결과 앞에 다가온 칠흑의 어둠은 자생력으로 벗어난 것이 아니라 미국, 중국, 소련이라는 외세의 협의로 일시에 다가왔으니, 이는 극심한 혼란의 지경을 초래한 것도 결국 우리 자신의 선택으로 귀결될 것이다.

이 과정의 불합리와 모순 그리고 반성의 목록으로 치부된 역사적인 사실이 중견 시인 고산지의 냉엄한 판단에 의해 서사시의 길을 재촉한다. 문학사에서 해방인 1945년 8월 15일에서 김일성의 남침인 1950년까지를 혼란의 시대로 정리한다. 이 시대의 정치적인 혼란은 이념의 대립으로 치달아 혼란이 극에 달했고, 결국 북은 소련의 사주를 받은 33세의 김일성이 권력을 장악했고, 남한은 이승만의 집권으로 정부 수립- 1948년을 기점으로 이데올로기가 서로

간에 대결로 치달아 강을 마주 보는 삿대질의 비극에 물살이 흐르고 있다.

해방은 빛나는 햇살이었지만 우리 자신이 가져오지 못한 죄업은 주로 고산지 시인이 추적하는 정치사의 일별一瞥이 아픔으로 노래된다.

4. 혼란으로 점철된 현대의 출발

우리 역사의 시대 구분은 근대와 현대라는 말이 때로 혼동된다. 왜냐하면, 역사가 짧다는 데서 오는 갈등이 담겨 있다는 점에서 분명하다. 그러나 한 가지 확실한 것은 근대 왕조의 몰락에서 이내 36년의 어둠을 지나 1894년 갑오개혁을 기점으로 현대라는 말이 생소하지만, 사실이기 때문이다. 고산지의 서사시 〈독립 없는 해방은 시리도록 아프다〉의 중요한 모멘텀이 시작되는 출발선이기 때문이다. 그 서두는 이렇게 시작된다.

조국祖國을 조국이라 주장하지 못하고
우리 말과 우리 이름을 빼앗긴 채

황국신민皇國臣民으로 살아온 36년 간의 고통을
그분이 보셨네, 그분이 들으셨네.

동해물과 백두산이 마르고 닳도록
보우하신 하나님이 큰일을 행하셨네.

꿈결 같이 찾아온 해방의 복된 소식
산천이 춤을 추고 돌들이 노래했네.

우리 혀가 풀리고
우리 입이 우리 이름 부르니

〈프롤로그〉 앞부분

우선 서사시의 제목부터 살핀다. 〈독립 없는 해방은 시리도록 아프다〉의 제목에서 느낄 수 있는 감성은 해방이 왔지만, 해방이 아닌 혼란을 암시하는 시어이고, 이로 인해 '아프다' 라는 말이 합리로 전개될 암시가 된다. 그러나 '시리도록' 에서는 잠시 주저의 생각이 다가선다. 부사 '시리다' 라는 말은 영어로는 cold이지만 우리말은 '차가운 것이 닿아서 춥고 얼얼하다' 또는 '괴롭고 힘들다' 는 의미를 공유한다.

결국, 해방은 아프다라는 말이지만 '독립 없는' 사연 때문에 반가운 해방은 아픔으로 귀결된다. 그렇다면 독립이 없는 해방은 외세에 갈가리 찢기면서 어렵게 세운 나라의 형편을 자조적自嘲的으로 표현한 논리인 셈이다. 왜 독립을 쟁취하지 못했는가는 결국 귀

납적인 반성문인 우리 자신의 힘이 없었다는 것과 외세의 틈새에서 희생양으로 살아야 할 숙명적인 아픔을 희화적戱畵的으로 표현한 셈이다.

고산지의 서사시의 내용은 자생적으로 쟁취하지 못한 혼란과 비극이 바로 우리 민족의 것으로 돌아오는 처절한 부메랑의 노래이다. 그 사건들의 기록이 매우 디테일한 전개와 치밀성에 그의 또 다른 문학적인 성과를 눈 여기게 된다

'프롤로그' 는 다소 의외의 전개로 보이는 부분이 "그분이 보셨네 그분이 들으셨네." 에서 직핍直逼보다는 우회迂廻로의 길을 표현한다. 왜냐하면, 종교적인 귀의로 모든 것을 귀착시킬 때, 결과는 '하나님이 보우하사' 로 만사가 해결될 것이기 때문이다. 그렇다면 종교 문학인가라는 의문이 다가든다. 내용을 읽으면 우리 자신의 부족으로 인해 좌, 우라는 극심한 이데올로기의 난장판을 연출한 것은 결국 누구의 탓인가 말이다.

왜, 나라를 빼앗겼고, 어찌하여 나라의 운명을 어질병으로 만들 때까지 하느님은 우리에게 무엇을 보우하셨는가? 나는 여기서 나라의 운명을 신의 영역으로 옮기는 것에 이의를 제기한다. 국민의 컨센셔스를 모을 수 있는 위대한 지도자의 부재와 국민의 의식에 비판 정신이 없는 부족을 탓할 때, 바른 해답이 나올 수 있기 때문이다. 현명한 국민은 현명한 지도자를 만든다는 명제에의 가난- 누란累卵의 위기에서 나라를 구한 영웅지도자는 많은 예로 거론할 수 있을

것이다.

5. 해방 전야의 혼란과 질서 구축

구한말舊韓末은 외세 앞에 자존의 문패를 걸 수 없는 주인 없는 집이었고, 힘없이 떠도는 표랑漂浪의 신세는 동가숙서가숙의 신세와 같았다. 일그러진 조선 왕조의 무기력은 급기야 지배 이데올로기였던 주자학 사상이 외부로부터 도전을 받자 기껏 나타나는 우물 안 위정척사 사상의 고함치는 이데올로기로 쪼그라든다. 정치적인 리얼리즘이 부국강병과 군사력의 중요성을 깨달았지만, 이미 기울어진 배를 곧추세우기에는 역부족이었다.

1592년 임진왜란과 병자호란이라는 미증유의 침략을 받고도 지도층은 아무런 대책이 없었기에 강대국의 먹잇감으로 전락하는 일은 이미 예견된 사실이었다. 여기서 서양 세력의 도전에 위정척사론의 시발은 천주교 박해와 미국의 제너럴 셔먼 호의 소각 사건 등에 이어 프랑스 함대의 침공으로 이어질 때, 쇄국鎖國 정책의 한계는 이미 수습할 수 없는 임계점에 이르렀다. 1910년 주권의 침탈에 나라를 헌납하는 비극 앞에 민족사의 수난은 길고 긴 어둠으로 들어갔고, 36년이라는 긴 기간을 지나 일시에 다가온 해방은 독립이기보다는 강대국의 잣대에 먹잇감으로 전락하는 참혹함이었다.

절망의 순간을 지나면 깨달음이 있어야 하겠지만 해방 이후의 형편은 분열과 외세의 사촉唆囑에 놀아나는 꼭두각시의 춤이 어설펐다. 고 시인의 서사시의 출발은 여기서 그의 생각이 시작된다.

압록강을 건너 두만강을 넘어
중국 대륙을 떠돌며
조국의 독립을 위해
일본군과 싸웠으나
우리의 힘으로는 나라 땅을
한 뼘도, 한 뼘도 수복할 수 없었네.

민족과 국가의 존립, 발전을 위해 인간이 존재한다는
전체주의 이념 아래 개인의 자유를 억압하는
나치즘과 파시즘, 일본의 군국주의와
민주주의 가치를 내세우며 싸웠던 연합국의
패전국敗戰國에 대한 전후戰後 처리 문제는
자본주의와 사회주의의 체제 대립으로 이어졌네.

국가간의 협상 기준은 정의正義가 아니였네.
자국自國 이익이 협상의 기준이였네.

〈해방전야〉에서

국가 간의 관계는 정의의 시대가 아니라 흥정과 이즘(ism)의 인력引力에 끌려 중심을 일탈逸脫한 시대의 표정이다. 압록강이나 두만강을 건너 풍찬노숙風餐露宿의 참담한 고난의 시절을 지나왔지만 힘없다는 탄식이 결론이었다. 해방은 결국 다가오는 걸음이었지만 우리 힘으로 얻은 것이 아니기에 무기력의 절망은 점점 우리끼리 혼란을 드러내는 길이 환히 열리고 있었음을 해방전야서 노래하고 있다.

"남한의 정치 세력은 민주주의적 보수 세력과
공산주의적 급진세력으로 양분되어 있다.
한민당을 중심으로 하는 보수 그룹은 서구 민주주의를 원하고
이승만과 임정의 환국을 희망하고 있다.
용공적 성향의 정치적 기회주의자 여운형이 이끌고 있는
급진파는 소련의 영향을 받고 있는 것 같다.
그들은 보수파에 비해 조직과 선전 활동면에서 앞서 있다."

기록하고 있네(09. 29.).

〈군정의 시작 – 2〉 중

칠흑의 어둠에서 맞이한 해방, 친탁과 반탁 등의 분열 대립은 남과 북으로 치달리는 서로 다른 생각의 일들이 지리한 욕망의 갈등이었고, 야망의 계절에 이합집산이 이루어졌다. 특이한 것은 군정 실시에 따라 기독교의 역할이 두드러졌고 선교사들에 의해 영명학교의 설립과 동량棟樑 양성에 일조했음을 기억해야 했다.

여운형의 기회주의와 민족 세력의 송진우, 김성수, 장덕수 등 많은 사람의 이름이 당시를 오르내린 지도층이었으니 시인은 이런 소용돌이의 시대상을 아주 면밀하게 추적하면서 비판의 칼날을 사용하고 있다. 문학은 어느 경우에도 살아 있는 사람을 위한 몫이기 때문에 모순 앞에서는 비판의 단호함이 있어야 한다면 시인 고산지의 역사 안목은 통찰에의 산물인 셈이다.

소련군의 지원을 받고 있던 김일성은

"북한 지역을 분리하여 먼저 공산화하고
공산화된 북한을 기지로 삼아 남한까지 공산화해야 한다.
이 계획을 효과적으로 진전시키기 위해서는
북한에 독자적 공산당이 조직되어야 한다."
고 주장했네.

〈군정의 시작 – 3〉 중

소련군 대위 김일성은 소련 꼭두각시의 역할을 충실히 수행하면서 야욕의 발톱을 갈아 북쪽을 비교적 진정시킨 이후 남한을 공산화하려는 음모의 치밀한 진행이 질서정연했다. 반면, 남한은 들끓는 세력 간의 쟁투에 혼란의 소용돌이로 영일寧日이 없었다. 5년의 신탁 통치를 반대하는 당시의 사회 상황을 유리알처럼 기록하는 고산지의 치밀한 분석력은 다음 글로도 알 수 있다.

김구는 임시정부의 긴급국무회의를 소집하여(12. 29.)
전 민족이 투쟁할 일만이 남아 있다고 선언했네.

안재홍 국민당 당수는 신탁 통치는
조선의 적화赤化 기도 공작이라며 총궐기를 선언했네(12. 29.)

인민당(이여성)은 신탁 통치는 외교로 투쟁해야 한다고 주장했네

임시정부를 중심으로 대시위 운동을 전개하자는 광복단은
“전쟁 없는 독립은 없고, 피 뿌리지 않는 자유는 결단코 없는 것이다. 나가자! 너 나 없이 피의 싸움 길로”
구호 아래 태극기를 들고

독립 만세를 부르며 나가자고 촉구했네(12. 29.)
요정과 바도 일제히 문을 닫고 신탁 통치를 반대했네

법무국 민, 형사과와 3법원과 3검사국 등 재야 법조인은
임시정부 명령에 절대복종하여
12월 29일 오후 2시, 총파업을 단행했네

〈신탁 통치 반대〉에서

소용돌이는 다른 소용돌이를 몰고 왔고, 해방공간은 혼란의 물결이, 해방의 기쁨이, 다시 서글픈 풍경화로 가슴을 짓누르고 있었다. 해방 이후 남한의 정당은 분열과 이합집산의 권력 쟁탈에서 일제의 잔재를 해소하고 민주주의를 건립하려는 기대보다 욕망에 나포된 민족주의자와 공산주의 자간의 권력 쟁투는 극심한 혼란의 터널을 지나야 했다. 우익의 분열은 심각한 양상이었다.

우여곡절의 군정이 마무리를 고하고 UN 한국 임시위원회에 의해 결정된 1948년 5월 10일 총선거일이 확정됨으로써 남한의 단독정부수립에 따른 우파 지도자 간의 정치적 분열은 가속의 페달을 밟았고, 1948년 7월 20일 이승만은 새로 제정된 헌법에 따라 대한민국 국회에서 초대 대통령으로 선출되었고, 1948년 8월 15일 대한민국 정부 수립이 완성되었다. 작금 문재인 정부는 이를 부정하고 있다. 이승만은 확고한 정신의 길을 선택하고 공산주의를 용납하지

않는 지도력을 보여주었으니, 다음 말로도 증거가 된다.

남한 전역을 돌면서 유세하는 이승만의 연설 주제는 언제나 똑 같았네.

"공산주의는 무서운 전염병인 콜레라와 같다.
공산주의와는 타협이나 협상이 불가능하다.
유일한 선택은 공산 독재주의에 굴복할 것인가,
저항할 것인가 하는 것뿐이다.
한국 민주주의를 구원할 수 있는 유일한 길은
신탁 통치와 공산주의를 철저히 거부하는 길뿐이다."

한국에 거주하는 많은 미국인들은 이승만의 캠페인에 박수를 보냈지만, 모스크바 신탁 통치 협정을 이행할 방법을 찾아야 하는 책임을 지고 있던 미 군정과 국무부는 분개했네

〈미소공동위원회〉중에서

"뭉치면 살고 흩어지면 죽는다." 절절한 호소와 "공산주의는 전염병과 같다."는 이승만의 말을 지금 돌아보면 과연 틀렸는가를 생각하게 한다. 역사는 가정법을 허용하지 않는다. 그러나 만약 이승만이 집권한 것과 김구가 집권한 것의 대비는 가능하다. 김구는 혁

명적인 성향이라면, 독립운동의 지도자는 될 수 있지만, 행정으로의 길은 더욱 험난할 수 있을지 모른다. 반면에 이승만은 유연한 정치가의 스타일이라는 말이 틀리지 않을 것이다. 그가 우리 민족의 주인공으로의 등장은 행운인지 모르는 일이다. 이는 오늘의 세계 10위권의 부강한 자유민주국가의 토대를 닦은 것을 부인할 수는 없기 때문이다.

이승만이 바라본 자유 정신은 공산주의를 절대 받아들일 수 없는 공고한 성주城主였다. 이런 정신이 제1공화국의 기반이었고 이후 이데올로기의 대립의 주인공은 이승만과 북한의 공산주의로의 야욕을 가진 김일성과의 두 이데올로기가 첨예한 양상이 평행선으로 진행된다.

독실한 크리스천인 이승만의 자유와 평화의 정신은 다음의 기도문으로 나타난다. 오늘에서 과거를 돌아보면, 칼 마르크스를 신봉한 공산 사상과의 대결에서 이승만의 선택이 옳았음을 역사가 증명한다는 사실이다. 국민을 잘 살게 하는 것이 정치의 요체이기 때문이라면, 우리는 누가 뭐라 해도 유사 이래 가장 잘 살고 있음을 부인할 수 없을 것이다.

5월 31일 오전 10시 20분, 감격적인 제헌 국회가 개원했네

최연장자인 이승만을 임시 의장에 추대했네

임시 의장 이승만은 개회사에 앞서

"대한민국 독립 민주국 제1차 회의를 여기서 열게 된 것을
우리가 먼저 하나님께 감사해야 할 것입니다.
종교, 사상 무엇을 가지고 있든지(대한민국 국민은)
누구나 오늘을 당해 가지고 사람의 힘으로만 된 것이라고
우리는 자랑할 수 없을 것입니다.
그러므로 하나님께 감사를 드리지 않을 수 없습니다.
나는 먼저 우리가 다 성심으로 일어서서
하나님에게 감사를 드리고자 합니다.
이윤영 의원 나오셔서 간단한 말씀으로
하나님에게 기도를 올려 주시기를 바랍니다."

〈유엔 한국임시위원단〉에서

이승만은 철저한 반공주의자요 자유 민주를 신봉하는 지성인이었다. 정치적인 야망 이전에 최남선의 신체시 〈해에게서 소년에게〉보다 10년 앞선 우국의 시 〈고목가〉를 노래한 선지적인 시인이었고, 시조를 좋아한 또는 한시漢詩에 조예를 가진 정치인이었다. 그의 절절한 기도는 충심이었고, 나라와 국민을 사랑하는 애민정신의 길이 형극의 길로 이어졌으니, 만약 그가 아니었다면 오늘날의 자

랑스러운 대한민국의 찬란한 경제 발전은 어려웠을 것이다. 이는 북한의 일당 독재의 공산주의에 신음하는 현상이 극명하게 증명하는 사실이기 때문이다.

해방 공간은 혼란이었다. 이는 4천 년 동안 왕조 국가의 신민으로 살아온 정신의 기조가 주자학이나 유교 정신에 철저한 바탕을 이해할 때라야 해답이 가능하다. 다시 말해서 세계사의 변화를 직시하지 못한 대원군의 통상 수교 거부 정책 – 외국 문물을 일찍 받아들인 일본과 달리 우리는 너무나 변화 앞에 무기력한 정신사가 있기 때문에 야욕으로 다가온 어둠의 일제 치하 36년을 불러들였고, 타의에 의해 다가온 독립은 독립이 아니라 어둠에 눈을 뜨지 못하는 혼란상의 가중을 가져왔다. 이런 결과는 극심한 삶의 고통을 국민에 가중加重시키는 눈물겨운 치하를 지나왔다.

다음 글은 일본 강점기의 빈민사貧民史를 쓴 강만길의 인용에서도 극명하게 드러난다. 요즘으로 치면 낯선 토막민土幕民, 화전민, 막일꾼 그리고 소작농 등의 실태 분석을 통해 얼마나 혹독한 가난의 벌판을 지나왔는가를 열거하고 있다.

초목의 뿌리나 잎새로 연명하는 사람이 얼마나 되는가 '보풀' 을 먹는 사람이 23,062호에 112,362명을 비롯하여 소나무 껍질, 머름, 칡뿌리 등 30여 종으로 살아가는 사람이 약 17만 3천 명인 즉 총인구의 6할이다.

〈동아일보 1924. 10. 12.〉

장수 지방 제북면 임평리에서는 세민들이 궁한 나머지 이곳 심곡산에서 나는 백토白土를 식용으로 하여 이 때문에 마을 사람 다수가 변비에 걸린 실례이다

1932년 전북경찰서가 조사한 〈세민細民의 생활 실태 조사〉

위의 글은 백성이 어떻게 살아왔는가를 증거가 되는 일례에 불과하다. 아울러 1930년대 나라를 찾기 위해 블라디보스토크나 상하이 등지로 유랑을 선택한 독립 운동가들의 눈물겨운 활동은 모두가 끓어오르는 애국의 정신적인 펼침이었다. 그러나 다가오는 해방과 눈부신 현상에 제대로 준비를 갖추지 못한 3년여의 혼란은 결국 고스란히 국민의 몫으로 다가오는 아비규환이었고, 정신사의 계획 부족은 결국 오늘까지 이데올로기의 포로가 되는 비극의 연장선으로 권력층에 비판 정신이 없는 것으로 정리된다.

다시 말해서 누천년 동안 순치馴致와 복종 사상의 유교儒教나 주자학의 신봉信奉의 결과로 볼 수 있을 것이다. 이런 견지에서 기독교의 정신이 서양 문화의 지주支柱 역할에서 피운 과학 우월의 결과로 나타난 부국의 현상과 동양의 정적靜的 권력 구축의 대비는 좋은 연구 대상이 될 것 같다. 동양의 사상은 정적靜的인 불교 문화와 유교가 중심이라면, 서양은 투쟁의 역사인 기독교의 과학 정신에서 동서東西 차이를 가른 원인이기 때문이다.

이를 직접적으로 거론하는 것은 아니지만 고산지의 서사시에 처

음과 마지막의 기도는 중요한 상징이자 암시가 된다.

해방解放이 곧 독립은 아니었네
독립獨立되지 못한 해방 공간은
냉전冷戰의 전초 기지가 됐네

정제精製되지않은 자유가
서로를 아프게 했네. 서로가 아팠네
독립 없는 해방은 시리도록 아팠네

4천 년 동안 왕권 통치에 길들여졌던 사람들
36년 동안 일제 식민지 치하治下를 거치면서
국권 회복國權回復을 외쳤지만

추구하는 국체國體는 저마다 달랐네

국민國民이 주인主人인 정치政治를
한 번도 체득體得해 보지 못했기에
소견所見대로 목청을 높였던 사람들

인민 민주주의를 추구하는 전체주의
사회 민주주의를 추구하는 사회주의

자유 민주주의를 추구하는 자본주의
우리의 의지와는 상관없이
우리의 운명은 지난 3년 동안
천국과 지옥을 넘나들고 있었네

나라 잃은 설움에 만주 벌판을
중국 대륙과 유라시아를 떠돌며
독립을 외쳤던 선구자들이 목 놓아 불렀던

"동해물과 백두산이 마르고 닳도록
하나님이 보우하사 우리나라 만세
무궁화 삼천리 화려강산
대한 사람 대한으로 길이 보전하세."

열강의 틈바구니에 낀 혼돈混沌 속에서

독립獨立은 되었으나
자립自立은 아직 할 수 없는
국민이 주인 된 나라, 드디어 탄생했네

상한 갈대 꺾지 않고
꺼져 가는 등불 끄지 않는

하나님의 은혜였네, 하나님의 역사였네

〈에필로그〉 전문

위의 기도는 시인 고산지의 나라 사랑의 열망을 대변한다. 비록 서사시의 구성상 리얼함을 필요로 하지만, 그 치밀한 전개 양상은 가히 자료의 방대함이나 각주脚註 56개를 살피면 압도당하는 것이 당연시된다. 물론 시를 읽는 재미와는 상관이 없는 점에서 고산지의 역량은 오불관언吾不關焉의 자세를 견지한다. 이는 옳은 일이다.

기도는 인간의 열정을 의미한다. 그 열정이 익어가는 것은 누가 주는 것이 아니라 자기의 신념으로 일으키는 놀라운 에너지의 법칙이기 때문이다. 이 점에서 고 시인의 정신에는 고갱이 정신이 투철하다. 이는 시인의 자유 정신과 신념의 줄기를 독자에게 전달하는 임무 – 독자는 깨달아야 한다. 다시 말해서 독자 또한 공부해야만 한다는 말을 하고 싶다. 좋은 작가는 좋은 독자에 의해 탄생된다는 말은 나변那邊의 의미가 결코 아니다.

6. 마무리에서

나는 고산지 시인을 볼 때면 놀란다. 시 구성을 위한 이미지의 치밀함에 한 번 놀라고, 유연한 정서의 묘사나 기술記述에서 다시 놀라고, 또 다시 서사시의 방대함과 정밀한 구성에 놀란다. 이는 인생의 다양한 경험, 사고의 깊이와 성찰省察의 산물이다. 고산지 시인은 의정부 영락교회의 장로로서 크리스천으로 살아가는 그의 진중한 삶의 모습과 아울러 정신의 기둥이 되는 기독교 사상을 눈 여길 때면 놀람이 사실로 확인된다. 그런 의미에서 고산지 시인은 향일성向日性의 문학 – 식물의 줄기가 햇볕이 강한 쪽으로 자라는 성질의 사고에서 정의와 신념의 자유인 – 을 추구하는 한국 문단의 귀중한 자산이라고 감히 말할 수 있다. *

독립 없는 해방은
시리도록 아프다

■

지은이 | 고산지

■

초판 1쇄 2018년 12월 17일

■

펴낸이 | 길명수
펴낸곳 | 배문사
출판등록 1989년 3월 23일, 제10-312호
주소 서울시 서대문구 경기대로 76
전화 (02) 393-7997
팩스 (02) 313-2788
e-mail pmsa526@empas.com

■

편집 인쇄 삼중문화사

ISBN 978-89-87643-68-7(03810)

값 15,000원

* 낙장 및 파본은 교환해 드립니다.